THE ART OF LEAD BURNING

LECTOR HOUSE PUBLIC DOMAIN WORKS

THE ART OF LEAD BURNING

C. H. FAY

ISBN: 978-93-89956-32-0

Published: 1905

LECTOR HOUSE LLP
E-MAIL: lectorpublishing@gmail.com

THE ART OF LEAD BURNING

A PRACTICAL TREATISE EXPLAINING THE APPARATUS AND PROCESSES.

BY

C. H. FAY

52 ILLUSTRATIONS.

Reprinted from
The Metal Worker, Plumber and Steam Fitter.

1905.

PREFACE.

The mystery which has always surrounded the work of the lead burner, like that of all other handicrafts outside of ordinary occupations, dissolves under the light of a full knowledge of the causes and effects that have a bearing upon it. While different works have treated on lead burning, it is the object of this special treatise to explain fully in detail every part of the apparatus and fixtures in common use, as well as their application, so that the careful reader may understand and acquire the art of lead burning by observing scrupulously the rules laid down and devoting sufficient time to practice to master it. This instruction, given by text and illustration, is only presented after the dangerous power of hydrogen gas when misused is thoroughly impressed on the reader. It would be well for all who hope to become lead burners to devote several evenings, with an interval between, to a thorough study of the chapters on hydrogen gas and its properties before taking any further steps. To those who have not had previous experience with chemicals and gases this preliminary study is indispensable for their own safety, for the successful operation of the apparatus and to insure satisfactory work. When fully familiar with the properties of hydrogen gas and the necessity of being careful when it is used little difficulty will be experienced in acquiring a full knowledge of the apparatus and fixtures. The art of burning the lead can only be acquired by practice, and either quickly or slowly, as the operator may be quick and skillful in acquiring any handicraft. In addition to describing what has been common practice for many years, the treatise contains a description of a new machine and burner which has only recently become available to lead burners. It also describes the method of lead burning with the use of illuminating gas and a soldering flux. A chapter is devoted to soft soldering and Britannia metal work, which is largely used in the equipment of bars and restaurants, the various joints being more easily made with a blow pipe than by any other method. As the workman who hopes to profit by reading this book can by a little negligence make a great deal of trouble for himself and others, caution and great care are advised whenever he is at work.

CONTENTS

CHAPTER I.

INTRODUCTION.

In compiling a treatise on the subject of lead burning too much stress cannot be laid upon the fact that the greatest care must be taken to observe the smallest details and to follow carefully every suggestion in regard to safety. I am aware of the responsibility resting upon me in placing this article into hundreds of hands, comparatively ignorant of the danger involved in handling so much hydrogen, without thoroughly instructing them in detail as to its use. I may be excused, therefore, if, for that reason, some of the explanations are so simple as to seem ridiculous; but my aim is to present to the trade a treatise that can be relied upon to be free from theory that has not been thoroughly tried and tested, so that the beginner can be sure that, if he follows directions as printed, nothing but satisfaction to him can result.

Study the Chapter on Hydrogen Gas.

I cannot too strongly recommend that the beginner study the chapter on hydrogen gas until the main points are memorized and clearly understood. The experiments should be performed and the result carefully noted for future reference before attempting to use the generator. It is time well spent to master the technical parts thoroughly before attempting the mechanical part. Then when a man takes up the mechanical he will do so with an intelligent understanding of what he is doing, and any little trouble which may then arise can be quickly overcome.

Another thing to be observed is to avoid nervousness. A nervous person cannot do this work with any degree of satisfaction, as it requires a cool head and a steady hand and a vast amount of patience to burn the upright and inverted seams.

Lead Burning Explained.

Lead burning is the process of fusing two pieces of lead together without the use of solder. The process consists in melting the edges together, a drop at a time, and when done with hydrogen gas and the blow pipe is called the "autogenous process." Lead can be fused with gasoline or illuminating gas by the use of the compound blow pipe; but, as ordinary gases give an oxidizing flame and require a flux, it is not considered a practical method.

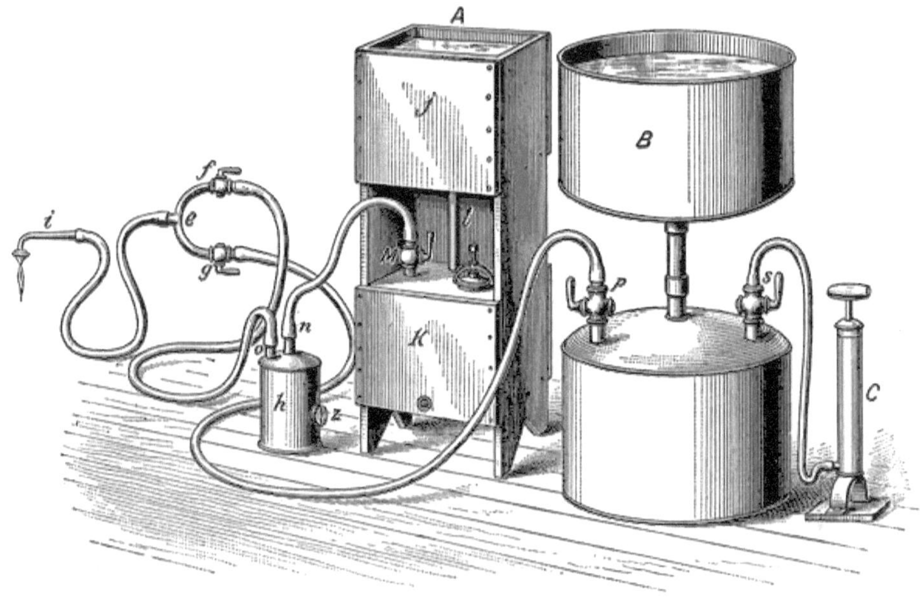

FIG. 1.—LEAD BURNING APPARATUS.

Lead is used extensively in lining tanks made to contain pickle dips, hot cyanide solution, storage batteries, acid tanks for manufacturing jewelry and water closet tanks, as water in many cases contains large quantities of lime and other deposits which rapidly destroy the solder used on copper linings. Tanks used for the above purposes must be lined with lead and the seams burned, as acids attack the tin in solders and destroy them. The demand for the work is rapidly increasing where it is introduced. I have demonstrated to many manufacturers that this is the cheapest method known, as it gives a permanent solution of the problem how to keep a chemical tank tight.

Method of Making Lead Lined Tanks.

The most common method resorted to in many large factories is to make the tanks out of very heavy cypress lumber, free from any knots or blemishes. The joints are carefully dovetailed and fitted together, and long bolts are used to draw the joints and keep them from leaking. Usually it takes from three to four days to complete one small tank, only to have it leak in a few months; whereas the same tank can be built in a few hours of any cheap lumber, and then, when it is lined with lead of a proper thickness and the seams burned it will usually last for an indefinite period, thereby saving floors and, many times, costly plating solutions.

The most common argument put forth by manufacturers is that the bottoms of lead lined tanks are soon cut out, owing to dropping sharp pieces of metal into them. This difficulty can be best overcome by placing a slatted bottom of wood in the tank, holding the same in place with strips of sheet lead, one end of which has been previously burned to the bottom of the tank. These strips are to be brought up through the slats and then bent over the top of them. This will keep the wood from floating, and is the only practical way to do it, as the false bottoms soon decay, and can be easily removed and replaced by simply bending back the strips of lead.

General Remarks.

Soft solder, as referred to here, means solder that melts at a temperature of 300 degrees or less, and is so called because of the low heat required to fuse the solder. It is used almost exclusively on the quick melting metals and compositions, such as block tin pipes and Britannia metal. It is also used by pattern makers in soldering white metal, as it requires but very little heat to sweat it through heavy articles. It should not be used to join any pipes which convey hot water or other hot liquids, as it is readily acted upon and destroyed. (The composition of these solders is explained in a special chapter.)

The chapters on blow pipe work, also on bar work, will alone turn many dollars into the pockets of the plumbers who have courage and ambition to acquire this line of work. Many times small leaks occur in difficult places that can be readily repaired by the use of the blow pipe and a common candle.

The lining of bars with Britannia metal is coming more and more into general practice, and it usually requires a specialist in this line to do the work. The soldering of this metal with a blow pipe and an alcohol torch is an easy matter, and is described in a special chapter.

There is no reason why this work should not be done by a plumber, particularly in small cities and towns, and to aid such as have not had the opportunity to familiarize themselves with such work I append such diagrams as may seem useful and necessary.

CHAPTER II.

THE APPARATUS.

The apparatus used for lead burning is illustrated in Fig. 1. It consists of a gas generator, A; an air holder, B, and pump, C; mixing fork, *e*, and necessary cocks, *f* and *g*; combined scrubbing cup and fire trap, *h*; blow pipe and tips, *i*.

The generator consists of an acid chamber, *j*, and a gas chamber, *k*. These are connected with an acid supply pipe, *l*, which conducts the acid from the acid chamber to the gas chamber, and also serves as a balance pipe.

This feature makes the generator automatic in its action, for as soon as the gas in the gas chamber gets up sufficient pressure, the acid in the gas chamber *k* is driven slowly back through the acid supply pipe *l* and up into the acid chamber *j*, where it is held until gas is used. When the acid descends and submerges the zinc more gas is generated, replacing that which has been used. This form of generator will never blow acid like the floating generator.

The requirements of a hydrogen generator for lead burning are that it should be safe, economical and automatic in its action. It must be so constructed that it will generate gas enough to keep the supply constant, and deliver it at sufficient pressure to keep the flame steady. It must also be provided with a combination fire trap and scrubbing cup. This will prevent the explosion of the generator by firing the gas in the hose. This trap must be partly filled with a solution of blue vitriol to act as a precipitation cup. (This is treated under the head of "Scrubbing Cup.")

The chief danger with an apparatus of this sort is its liability to accident by the careless use of the gas, and, as a mixture of hydrogen and air is very explosive, great care must be taken to exhaust all the air in the generator and tubes before attempting to light the gas at the blow pipe. The only way to make sure that the air is exhausted is to test the gas, as described under the head of "The Flame and Its Management."

A Few Cautions.

It is a very sensible idea to keep spectators away from the generator, as they are very apt to strike matches or tread on the tubes, in spite of warnings to be cautious, for if there should be a leak, even so slight as to be hardly detected, it would cause a violent explosion, and as hydrogen is both odorless and colorless, this could easily happen without being noticed. This is probably the origin of the apparent secrecy with which a lead burner usually surrounds himself.

If an explosion should occur in the tubes and they should catch fire, the operator must have presence of mind enough to reach the gas cock on the generator and close it. If gas explodes in the generator, all that can be done is to dodge the flying pieces and make a new generator. If such an incident should occur and vitriol should spatter on the person doing the work, or his assistant, a solution of bicarbonate of soda or common washing soda should be at once applied to the wounds. If that cannot be procured, grease or oil of some kind should be used without delay, rubbing it on the spots where the acid burns, and this will neutralize the acid and so prevent it doing further damage. There should be no trouble of this sort in the hands of a careful workman. The watchword should be, "Test the gas before using." If this is done, explosions will never occur.

CHAPTER III.

HYDROGEN GAS.

This element was discovered by Cavendish in 1766, and was called by him inflammable air. The name hydrogen is derived from two Greek words, one signifying "water" and the other "to generate," on account of its forming water when burnt. It occurs in its free state in the bases of volcanoes, and by the aid of the spectroscope has been detected in the sun and stars. It chiefly exists in combination with oxygen as water, and is an important constituent of all vegetable and animal substances.

Hydrogen is obtained by the decomposition of water in various ways. On a large scale, nearly pure hydrogen may be prepared by passing steam over charcoal, or coke, heated to a dull redness. If the temperature be kept sufficiently low hydrogen and carbon dioxide will be the sole products, and the latter may be removed by causing it to traverse a vessel filled with slaked lime, but if the temperature be allowed to rise too high, or an excess of air be admitted, carbon monoxide is also produced, and cannot be removed from the mixture.

Pure hydrogen is a colorless, odorless, transparent and tasteless gas, and has never been liquefied. It is very slightly soluble in water. It is the lightest of all known bodies and is not poisonous, although it cannot support life, and if mixed with a certain proportion of oxygen it can be breathed for a considerable length of time without inconvenience. It is highly inflammable, and burns in the air with an almost colorless, nonluminous flame, forming water. A burning taper is extinguished when plunged into hydrogen, and all bodies which burn in the air are incapable of burning in hydrogen.

Hydrogen does not spontaneously enter into reaction with any of the elements, although it has a powerful affinity for several of them. Thus, when hydrogen and oxygen are mixed nothing occurs, but if a lighted splint is introduced a violent explosion ensues, water being produced. Similarly chlorine and hydrogen are without action upon each other in the dark, but if the mixture is exposed to a bright light, or if heated by the passage of an electric spark, the gases are at once combined with explosive violence, forming hydrochloric acid.

Hydrogen is usually prepared by the action of zinc or iron on a solution of hydrochloric or sulphuric acid. All metals which decompose water when heated readily furnish hydrogen, on treatment with hydrochloric or sulphuric acid. Many other metals enter more or less readily (although none so readily) into reaction with these acids. Also, many other acids than sulphuric or hydrochloric acids may be used, but none acts so quickly. In all cases the action consists of the displacement of the hydrogen of the acid by the metal employed, and if the acid is not one which can enter into reaction with the displaced hydrogen, the latter is also evolved as gas.

If pure gas is required it is necessary to employ pure zinc or iron, as the impurities in the ordinary metal communicate an extremely disagreeable odor to the gas.

The pure gas is not absolutely essential for lead burning, and owing to their being much cheaper, and also on account of their increased quickness of action, the commercial qualities of sulphuric acid and zinc are employed in the generator described.

The commercial zinc is known as spelter and is sold in pigs or blocks, which are easily broken into fragments, like stove coal, with a heavy hammer. The commercial sulphuric acid is known as oil of vitriol and is sold by the pound. The acid cannot be employed in its pure state, but must be reduced with water in the proportion of one part of acid to seven parts of warm water. They must be mixed by adding the acid slowly to the water; never the water to the acid. The combination of acid and water enters at once into reaction and always generates heat, and the result of adding water to acid would be small explosions. There would be danger of the acid flying on one's clothes or into the eyes. The mixture should never be stronger than six parts of water to one of acid.

The beginner will observe from the above that the generator cannot be crowded by making the acid solution strong. Hydrogen is a peculiar gas and also a dangerous one for one ignorant of its peculiarities to experiment with, and in order to thoroughly understand it the following experiments should be demonstrated, which can be done with little expense. The beginner should note the result of each experiment as demonstrated, and carefully commit the same to memory for future reference.

Experiment 1.

Test for Hydrogen. — Fill a small jar or wide mouthed bottle with hydrogen. This is done by first filling the bottle with water, inserting the end of the tube from the hydrogen generator, having first exhausted the air in the tube, then quickly inverting the bottle and placing the neck, Fig. 2, in a pan of water (A); the water will stay in the bottle. Now turn on the hydrogen. The gas, being lighter than water, will rise to the top of the bottle (B), drive out the water, and replace it with pure hydrogen, which should be free from air. Remove the bottle from the pan of water, keeping it inverted. Thrust a lighted splint into the bottle. The gas will light and burn at the mouth of the bottle. If the splint is thrust far into the bottle it will go out. Drops of water collect in the bottle. Burning is a union with oxygen; therefore, the burning of the hydrogen shows that it has an affinity for oxygen. The splint goes out because the hydrogen does not support combustion. *If no air is allowed to get into it the gas cannot burn or explode.*

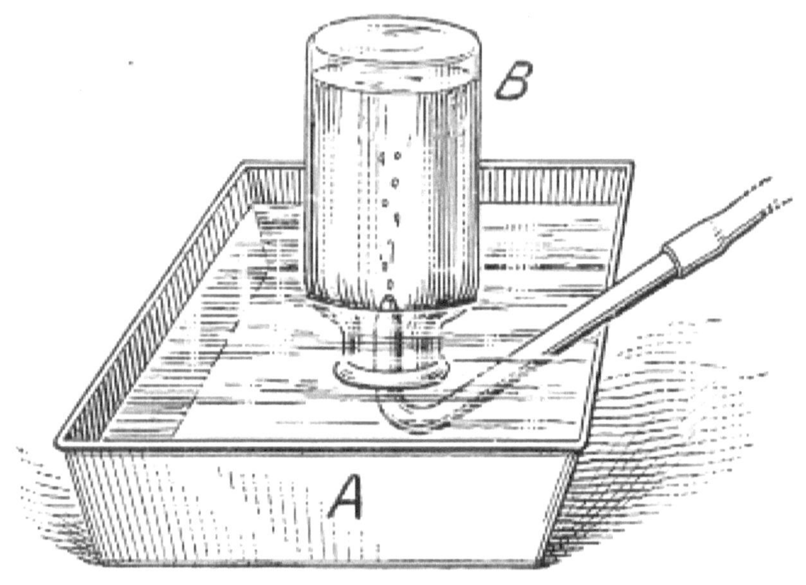

FIG. 2.—EXPERIMENT NO. 1.

Experiment 2.

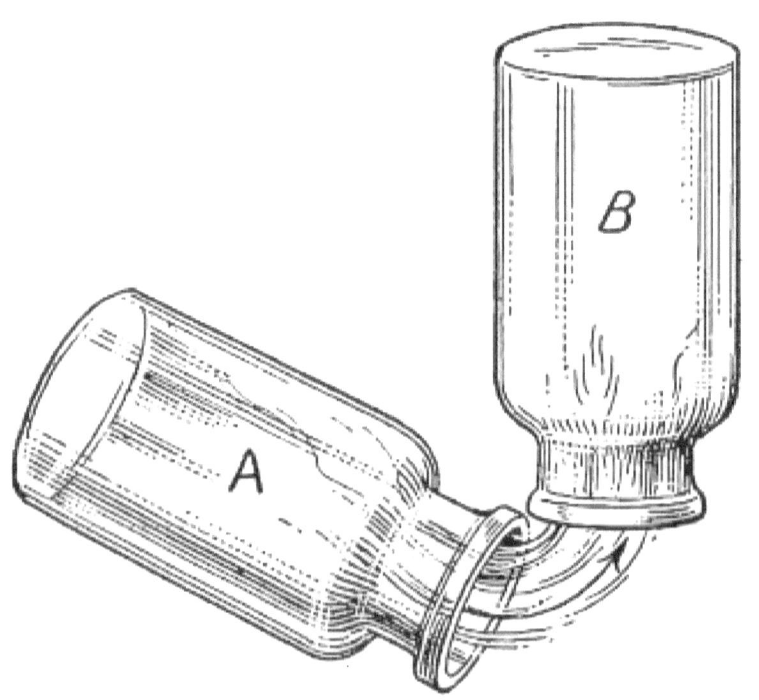

FIG. 3.—EXPERIMENT NO. 2.

Proving That Hydrogen is Lighter Than Air.—Bring an inverted bottle of hydrogen close to an empty bottle, also inverted, Fig. 2. Gradually tip the bottle containing hydrogen (A) until it is brought to an upright position beneath the empty bottle. Test the bottles for hydrogen. The hydrogen will be found in the bottle (B) that was at first empty, proving that *hydrogen is lighter than air*, as it has risen in the empty bottle, displacing the air that was in it. If the bottle of hydrogen is left in an upright position without a cover for a few moments the gas will entirely disappear.

Experiment 3.

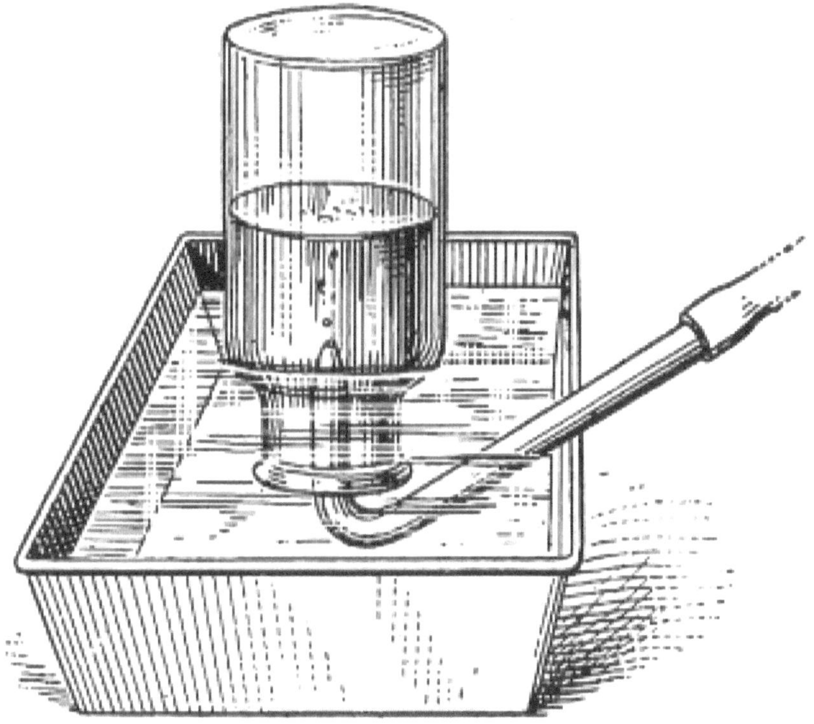

FIG. 4.—EXPERIMENT NO. 3.

The Effect of Mixing Hydrogen and Air.—Half fill a bottle with water and invert it in a pan of water, Fig. 3, leaving the upper half filled with air. Displace the air in the bottle with hydrogen, then thrust a lighted splint into the bottle, and the gas will light with an explosion. When the bottle was half filled with water the other half was air. The hydrogen took the place of the water, so that the bottle contained equal quantities of hydrogen and air. When the hydrogen was lighted it combined with the oxygen in the air. The union of the two gases caused the explosion, proving that the combined gases are very explosive.

Experiment 4.

To Make Hydrogen From Water.—Drop a piece of potassium into a little water and cover it. The potassium floats on the water and soon burns. Potassium acts vigorously on cold water, setting free hydrogen, and unites with parts of it to form "caustic potash."

CHAPTER IV.

THE CONSTRUCTION OF THE GENERATOR.

The construction of the generator is the first step in the mechanical part of the business, and to simplify this a complete set of reference drawings has been constructed and is herewith given. The assembling of the parts should be clear, with the assistance of the perspective drawing of the completed apparatus, and any mechanic of ordinary ability should be able to construct this generator without any trouble. The following bill of material should first be purchased:

> One ⅞-inch whitewood board 10 inches wide and 8 feet 6 inches long.
> One ½-inch whitewood board 12 inches wide and 4 feet 6 inches long.
> One piece of 6-pound sheet lead 3 feet wide and 6 feet 6 inches long.
> Three ⅛-inch female hose end gas cocks.
> One piece of ⅛-inch brass tubing 2 feet long.
> One foot of ¼-inch lead pipe.
> One 4-inch charging screw.
> One 1¼-inch cleaning screw.

Making the Charging and Cleaning Screws.

These goods can be readily purchased from dealers, with the exception of the charging and cleaning screws. They can be made in any brass foundry. The only difference between the charging and cleaning screws is the size. The charging screw, Fig. 5, should be at least 4 inches in diameter, or large enough to pass the hand through, while the cleaning screw should be 1¼ inches in diameter, or large enough to pass over a 1-inch pipe. A piece of sheet lead is fitted into the cover, as shown at *a*, to protect the metal from the acid. Soft putty is used for a packing, as shown in Fig. 5.

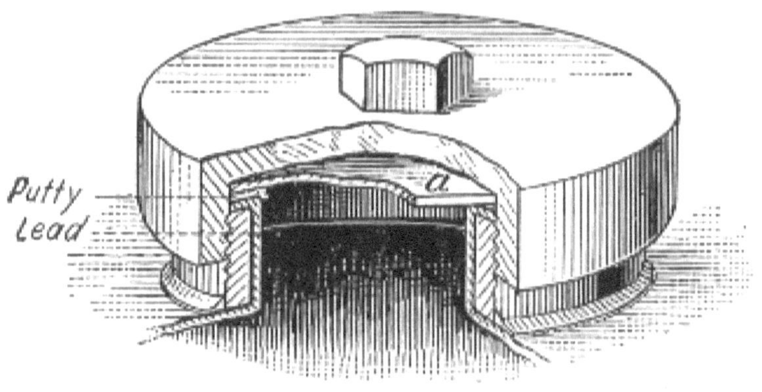

FIG. 5.—THE CHARGING SCREW.

The best, although a more expensive, charging screw is shown in Fig. 6. As will be seen from the cut, it consists of a base, k; cover, d; clamp, e, and screw, f. The base is simply a plain iron or brass ring, 4 inches in diameter, ⅛ inch thick and 1 inch high. The bottom is to be faced smooth, while the top is recessed 3-16 inch deep to receive the sheet lead and packing of putty, as at a. Two nubs, b and b, are cast on opposite sides, as shown, to act as grips for the clamp c. These nubs are ¾ inch long and project out from the body of the base ¼ inch, and are made sufficiently strong to stand the strain of the screw. The cover d is made of the same material as the base, the center being raised, as shown, to give it strength. Cast directly in the center and on the top is the nub e, ⅝ inch high and ⅝ inch in diameter. This is drilled to receive the ⅜-inch screw f. A groove 1-16 inch wide and 1-16 inch deep is cut all around the bottom of the screw, as shown at i. A hole is then drilled through the side of the nub e, and in line with the slot i. A pin can then be driven through the hole and will pass through the slot i, making a swivel joint that will connect the cover and screw together. The screw f is made of ⅜-inch round iron sufficiently long to give an action of about 1 inch. The top at n is filed square to receive a wheel such as is used on a common gate valve. A long thread should then be cut on this screw. The clamp c is made a half circle in shape, so as to clear the cover with ease. It should be ¾ inch wide, flat on the under side, while the top side should have a rib cast on it to prevent springing. The top at g should be reinforced with metal and made heavy enough to stand drilling and tapping to receive the screw f. A wood pattern can be made for these parts, and they can then be molded in any brass or iron foundry. In making the patterns they should be cut down as much as possible, so as to make the finished article as light as is consistent with the strength required. The same directions will answer for the cleaning screw. The hole to receive the sheet lead over the cleaning screw should not be over 1½ inches in diameter, and the rest of the screw should be made in proportion to this hole. The advantage of this screw over others is that it does not wrench the sheet lead in making it up, and, owing to its construction, it is always sure to make a tight joint without straining the generator.

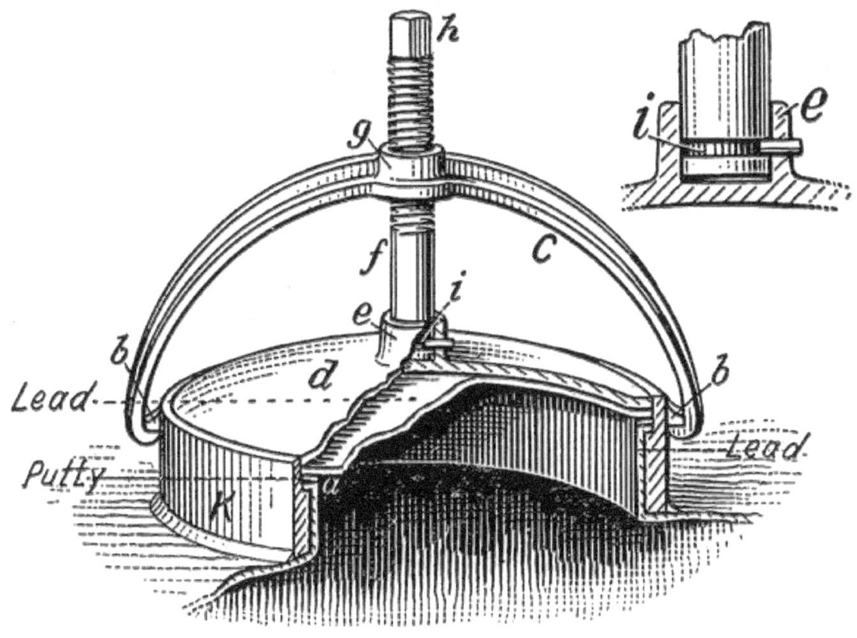

FIG. 6.—THE BEST CHARGING SCREW.

Building the Frame.

The frame can be made of galvanized iron, but wood is much superior, as it retains the heat generated in the gas chamber much better. To make the frame take the ⅞-inch board and cut off two pieces, 10 inches square, A and B in Fig. 8; 5 inches from one side and 2 inches from the back of one of these pieces bore a 1½-inch hole, C, and countersink it. This is for the acid supply pipe to pass through. These pieces are intended for shelves upon which to rest the acid and gas chambers. Cut the remaining board into two pieces 38 inches long. Lay these two boards together. Five inches from the side and 3 inches from the bottom bore a 1½-inch hole, *d*. Then saw out a V-shaped piece, Fig. 7. This will form the legs of the generator.

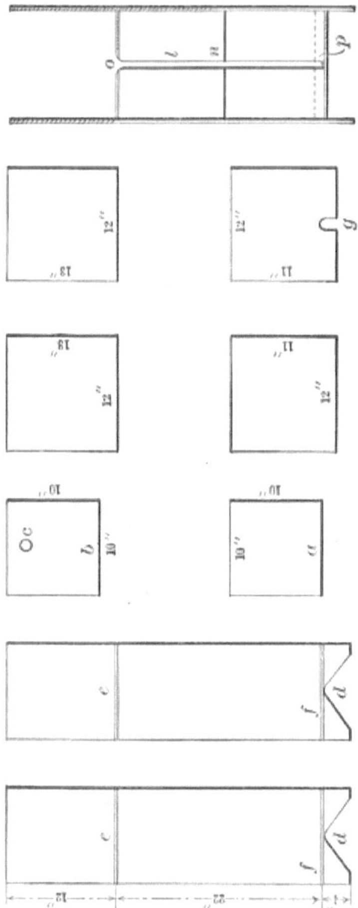

FIG. 7.—MAKING THE ACID CHAMBER.

Take a square, and 12 inches from the top of these boards draw the lines *e* and *e*. Twenty-two inches below these lines draw the lines *f* and *f*. These lines represent the tops of the shelves. The shelves should be nailed or screwed into place. The shelf B should be placed on the top, keeping the hole C to the back. Take the ½-inch board and cut two pieces to measure 12 × 13 inches and two pieces 11 × 12 inches. These form the sides of the acid and gas chambers. The two 12 × 13 inch boards form the sides of the acid chamber and the 11 × 12 inch boards the sides of the gas chamber.

Directly in the center and 1¾ inches from the bottom of one of the 11 × 12 inch boards bore a 1½-inch hole. The remaining piece should be sawed out, leaving a hole at *g*. This is so that the board can be removed in case of a leak without disturbing the cleaning screw. These pieces should be fitted to their places with round head screws, and if properly done will form an acid chamber which will measure 10 × 10 × 12 inches, and the gas chamber will measure 10 × 10 × 10 inches. The acid chamber must be larger than the gas chamber, to allow the full charge of acid to be used without overflowing.

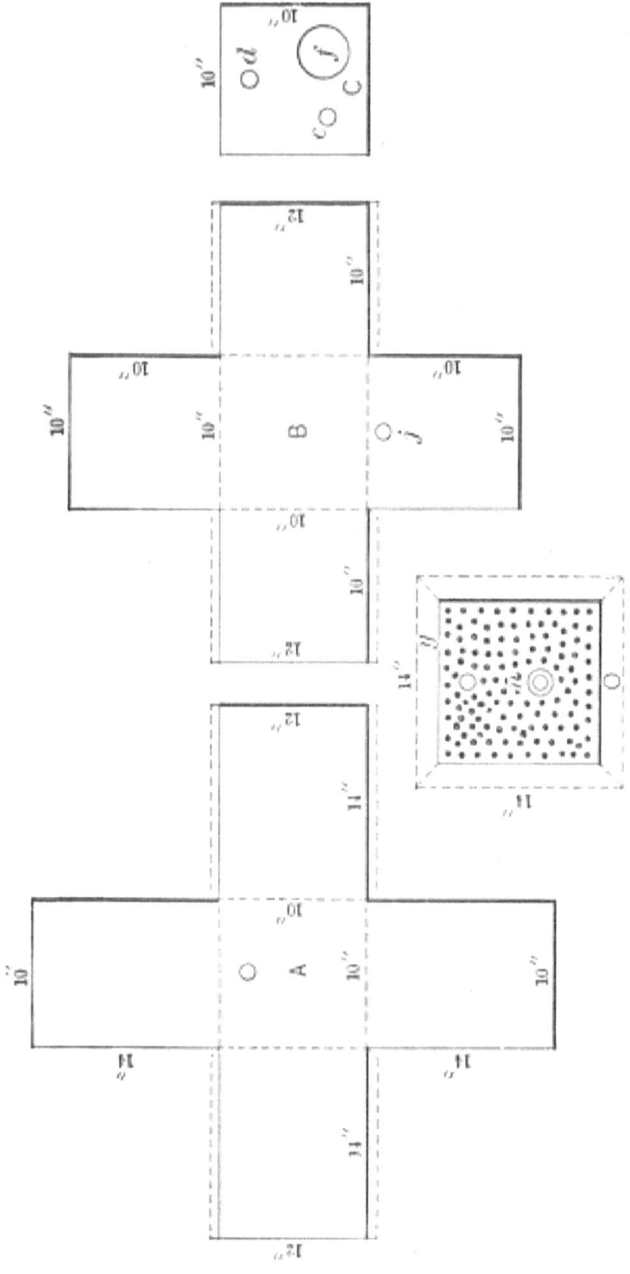

FIG. 8.—MAKING THE SHELVES AND THE PERFORATED BOT-
TOM.

Now fit the sheet lead. Six-pound is plenty heavy for this generator and will last a lifetime. Cut it as shown in Fig. 8, A and B. Form the lead so that the seams when finished will come on the outside, as in case of a leak in a seam it can then be easily repaired by removing one of the boards. The projecting edges of lead should be dressed over the edges of the top to protect the wood from the acid, but do not fasten them, as the tanks will have to be removed and the seams burned.

Now cut the piece of lead C to form the top of the gas chamber. None is needed for the acid chamber, as it must be left open so that no resistance will be offered to the action of the gas on the acid. Five inches from the side and 2 inches from the back of this piece cut a hole, *d*, Fig. 8, 1¼ inches in diameter, and dress it up with the bending iron to 1½ inches in diameter, taking care to preserve the thickness of the metal. This is for the acid supply pipe to pass through.

Three inches from the side and 3 inches from the front cut a ⅛-inch hole, *e*. This is the gas outlet. Three and one-half inches from the opposite side and 4 inches from the front cut the hole *f*, 2¾ inches in diameter. Dress this up and over the flange of the charging screw *a*, Fig. 6. This may seem a difficult thing to do, but lead must be worked slowly. Heating the lead while dressing it will help wonderfully. If it is not possible to make a good job in this manner, then cut the hole 4 inches in diameter and burn in a collar sufficiently big to dress over and cover the flange of the screw. This is to prevent acid from coming into contact with the screw and destroying it. Treat the cleaning screw in the same manner. The location of this screw is in the center and as close as possible to the bottom of the gas chamber, as shown in Fig. 8 at *j*.

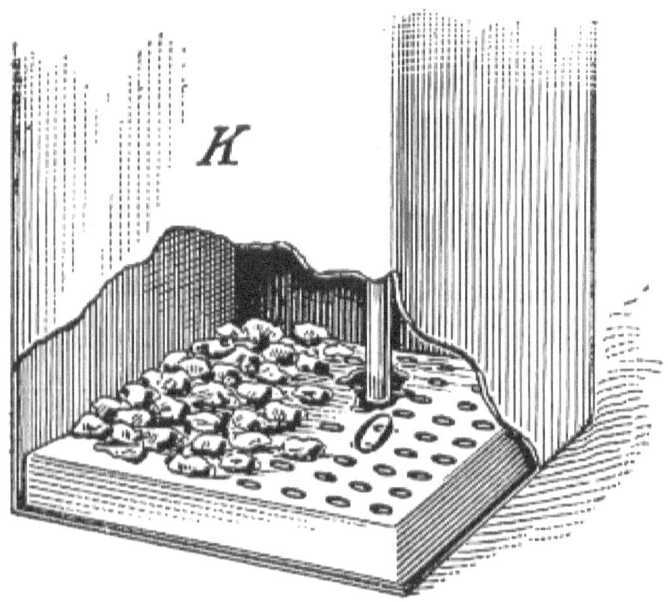

FIG. 8½.—SHOWING THE PERFORATED SPELTER SHELF IN PLACE IN THE GENERATOR.

It is necessary to have a false perforated bottom in the gas chamber to rest the zinc upon and also to keep it above the solution. To make and support this bottom take a piece of sheet lead 14 inches square, as shown in Fig. 8, and form it in the shape of a pan, which will drop easily into the gas chamber k, Fig. 8½. A piece of 1½ or 2 inch lead pipe, 2 inches long, n, should be burned on the center of the false bottom, to prevent the center from sagging with the weight of zinc. Then punch the bottom O, Fig. 8, full of ¼-inch holes. A 1½-inch hole, y, should also be cut in line with the holes for the acid supply pipe.

Remove the tanks and burn the seams. Place the tanks back in place. Then take a piece of the ⅛-inch brass pipe, 1½ inches long. Cut a thread on one end, tin the other end, and burn it to the top of the gas chamber at e; also the collar for the charging screw. Then place the perforated bottom in the gas chamber, taking care to keep the holes for the acid supply pipe in line. Do not make any mistake in putting in this bottom. Its use is to act as a shelf to hold the zinc, and if put in properly it will hold the zinc about 2 inches above the real bottom. The top of the gas chamber c should then be burned in. Now by measuring find the exact length of the acid supply pipe, Fig. 7, i. This pipe should extend from the bottom of the acid chamber o to the bottom of the gas chamber p, as shown in Fig. 7. From one end of this pipe several V-shaped pieces should be cut, p, about 1 inch deep.

This is one of the most particular parts of the apparatus, as this is where the automatic action comes in, and great care must be taken in cutting these holes not to have any of them come closer to the perforated bottom than 1 inch. If this were not observed the acid would be constantly in contact with the zinc, and would rapidly get up pressure of gas sufficient to blow acid out of the upper tank, and the extra gas would escape through the acid supply pipe in blows. In fact, it would make the generator useless. This is the trouble with the French apparatus. The acid, having no place to expand in, is constantly coming into contact with the zinc, and unless the gas is being used as fast as generated it will blow acid out of the acid holder, making a bad mess, besides being very wasteful.

Now flange the other end of this pipe to fit the countersunk bottom of the acid chamber. Place the pipe in position and burn it to the bottom of the acid chamber and to the top of the gas chamber n, Fig. 7. One of the ⅛-inch gas cocks should be screwed on the brass nipple on top of the gas chamber. This will complete the gas generator. It will make a better job if the back of the generator be boarded tight and a door made to fit the space between the bottom of the acid chamber and the top of the gas chamber in front. It is very convenient to have it fixed in this manner, as in shipping it from one point to another the tubes and other incidentals can be placed in the space so made and shipped with safety. There is no objection to the acid and gas chambers being made in the shape of cylinders, instead of square, if so desired, but if made circular they should be made to fit the frame tightly to prevent jarring and eventually breaking the seams.

CHAPTER V.

MAKING THE GAS TO BURN THE GENERATOR.

In towns supplied with illuminating gas it is a comparatively simple operation to burn the lead lining for the generator, but for the convenience of those who cannot obtain gas it is necessary to give some method by which the generator can be burned. The method described will answer for illuminating gas as well as for gasoline.

To generate gas from gasoline is a simple operation. To do this, take a common 1-gallon oil can, remove the top of can screw and punch a ¼-inch hole in the center of it. Then make a tube of tin that will pass through this hole, sufficiently long to extend half way to the bottom and project 2 inches outside of can screw, and solder this tube in place. This projecting tube is for the purpose of connecting to the air holder. Remove the spout of the can and replace it with one to which the hose can be connected. Now fill the can two-thirds full of gasoline, but not full enough to cover the gas outlet, else it would be likely to force gasoline out instead of gas.

After this is done, screw the can screw in place, the long end of the tube extending into the gasoline, as shown in *j*, Fig. 9. A hose connection is now to be made with an air holder. As it is necessary to have an air holder both for this process and the hydrogen gas process, methods will be described for making air holders which can be used for either.

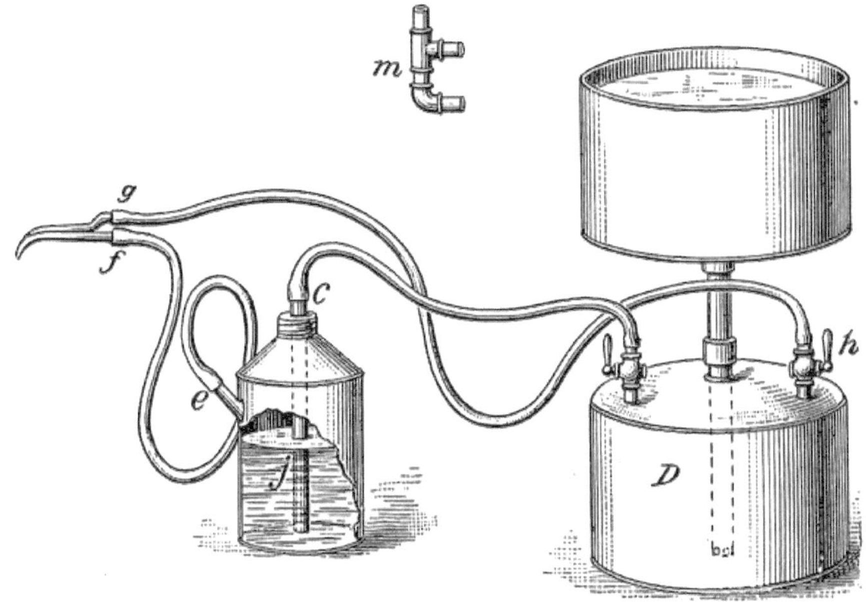

FIG. 9.—GAS APPARATUS FOR BURNING THE GENERATOR.

Air Holders.

Different lead burners have different views on this subject. Some prefer the bellows, with a contained air holder; some the air holder built like a gasometer, while others use an air holder similar to the generator in construction. These all have their advantages. For my part, I own and use all three.

The advantage of the bellows is that it can be easily transported and does the work perfectly, but it requires constant pumping, which soon tires the helper, and for that reason could not be used on jobs requiring more than four or five hours' labor.

The gasometer style of air holder is the easiest to use, if one does not employ a helper and has a large amount of work to do. The pressure can be regulated to suit the work by placing one or more weights upon it until the desired pressure is obtained. It does not require pumping up more than three or four times a day, which is its principal virtue. It is a perfect shop apparatus. Its disadvantage is that it requires a large quantity of water to fill it, which is not always available, and when full it is so heavy that it requires a truck to move it around.

By far the best air holder is the one shown as part of the apparatus in Fig. 9, and illustrated separately in Fig. 10. This only requires a few pails of water to fill it, and the exact pressure of the gas can be had by building it the same hight as the hydrogen gas generator. It does not require constant pumping, and I recommend this air holder for general use, as possessing more advantages, with less trouble, than any other air holder in use. However, all three will be described, and the beginner can make the one most suited to the material available.

Air Holder No. 1.

The beginner will notice in Fig. 10 that this air holder is so constructed that it gets its air pressure direct from the head of water, and also that this pressure can be varied by making the connecting piece of pipe longer or shorter, as may be desired. Of course, the pressure will vary slightly as the water descends into the air chamber, but not enough to make it objectionable, as it will be the helper's duty to watch the water line and renew pumping as often as the water falls below a certain point.

To make this holder, a tank, *a*, Fig. 10, 12 inches high and 18 inches in diameter, should be constructed of galvanized sheet iron. On this tank double seam a flat bottom. The top must be raised slightly, as shown, to give it strength. This can be done with the raising hammer, or it can be done by making the circle for the top ¾ inch larger than the bottom, then making a cut to the center. It can then be drawn together and riveted in any desired pitch. A hole must be punched in the center of this top large enough to receive a 1-inch galvanized pipe, *b*. Six inches apart and 2 inches from the edge punch two holes, *c* and *d*, large enough to receive pieces of ⅜-inch galvanized pipe. This top should then be fitted and placed on the body of the tank.

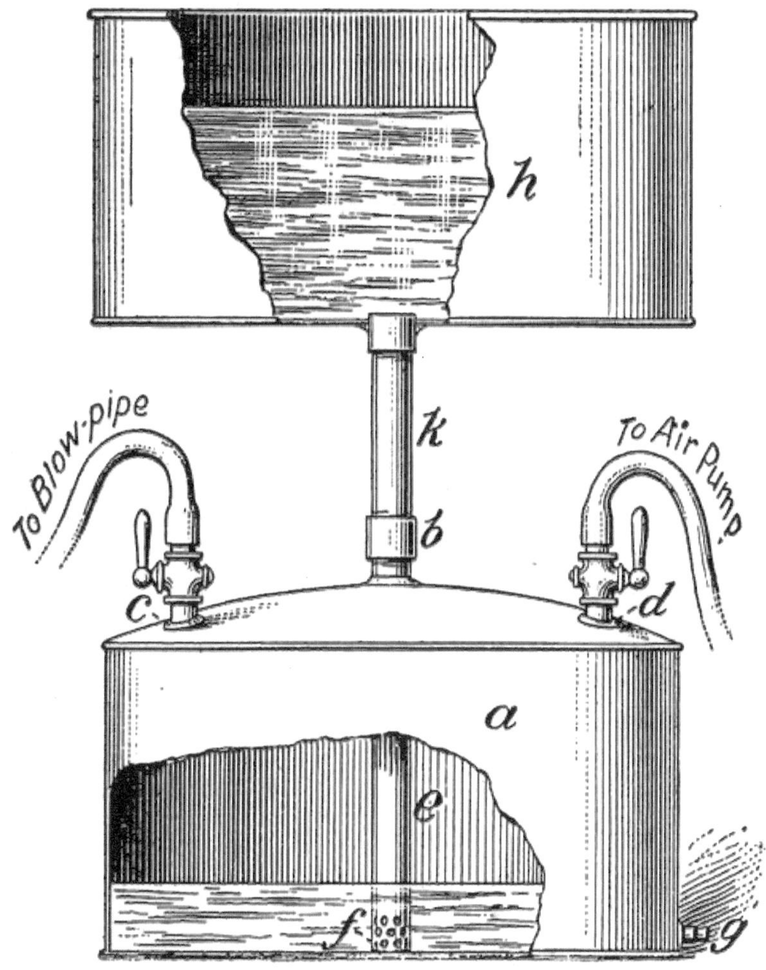

FIG. 10.—AIR HOLDER NO. 1.

Take a piece of 1-inch galvanized pipe, *e*, sufficiently long to touch the bottom and projecting 1 inch out of the top of the tank, cut a thread on the projecting end and drill the other end full of ¼-inch holes, *f*, to the hight of 1 inch, to allow the water to flow freely. This pipe rests on the bottom of the lower tank and carries the weight of the upper tank. Solder this pipe in place. Then take two ⅜-inch nipples, 1 inch long, and solder them into their places, and on these nipples screw two ⅜-inch hose end gas cocks, *c* and *d*. One of these cocks is for the purpose of connecting to the air pump, and the other to the mixing cock. As close as possible to the bottom of the tank solder in a ½-inch coupling, *g*. Into this coupling screw a plug. This is for the purpose of draining the tank when out of use.

Now make another tank, *h*, 19 inches in diameter and 11 inches deep, the top to be left open and wired with a heavy wire. Double seam a flat bottom on this tank. Directly in the center of this bottom punch a hole large enough to receive a 1-inch coupling. Then cut a 1-inch coupling in half and solder it into this hole, putting the thread side down and leaving it as near flush with the outside of the tank as possible, so that if it is desired to move the air holder to and from a job it can be taken apart and the lower tank nested in the upper tank, making a compact bundle and reducing the danger of damage by careless handling.

To connect these tanks, all that is required is a piece of 1-inch iron pipe, *h*, 12 inches long, with a coupling on one end. To operate this air holder, close the two air cocks on the lower, or air, tank; then fill the upper tank nearly full of water, taking care not to put too much in it, or it will overflow the lower tank and get into the tubes, and if this happens the tubes will have to be removed and hung up to dry, or drops of water will be blown into the blow pipe and extinguish the flame. It is then ready for use. The air in the air chamber is compressed by the weight of the water in the upper tank, and if the water line is at the same hight as the acid line in the hydrogen gas generator the pressure of air must be the same as the pressure of gas. As air is used the water descends through the pipe and will gradually fill the lower chamber. It can then be forced back into the water chamber by attaching the air pump to the cock *h* in Fig. 9, or *d* in Fig. 10, without disturbing the gas or in any way interfering with the operator. To connect with the cock *h* in Fig. 9 it is only necessary to disconnect one line of hose and connect the pump; then close the other cock and work the pump until air bubbles up in the upper tank; then shut the cock, remove the pump and connect the hose to the gasoline can, open the cocks and the apparatus is ready for use.

Air Holder No. 2.

To make the air holder shown in Fig. 11, take a sheet of No. 26 gauge galvanized iron 30 inches wide. Make it into a cylinder 26 inches in diameter, double seam a flat bottom on it, and wire the top with ¼-inch iron rod, which will make it stiff enough to withstand the pressure of water. Close to the bottom and 3 inches apart punch two holes, *a* and *b*, large enough to receive ⅜-inch galvanized pipe couplings. Solder these couplings in place.

On the inside of this tank and into these couplings screw two pieces of ⅜-inch pipe 4 inches long with elbows pointing straight up. Into these elbows screw two pieces of ⅜-inch pipe long enough to come flush with the top of the tank F. On the outside of the tank and into the ⅜-inch couplings screw two ⅜-inch nipples 2 inches long, and on these nipples screw two ⅜-inch hose end gas cocks.

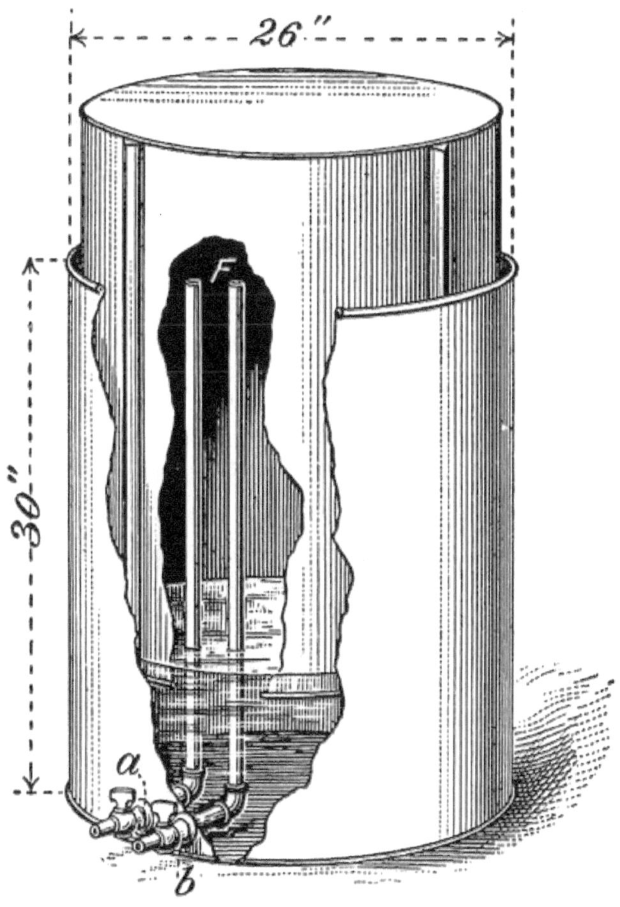

FIG. 11.—AIR HOLDER NO. 2.

Now, with the same sized sheet iron, make another tank 2 inches smaller in diameter than the first tank. This should have a flat bottom, and be wired as previously described. Then take four strips of sheet iron 30 inches long and 2 inches wide, and form each into V shape lengthwise. Lay off the circumference of this tank in four equal spaces. One side of the V-shaped pieces should then be soldered on at each space. The other side should be left loose to allow for adjustment. These pieces form the guides to the upper tank and prevent it from tipping sideways and binding. Two of the guides are shown in the illustration, Fig. 11.

The lower tank should now be filled about one-third full of water. The upper tank should then be inverted and placed in it. The air pump must then be connected to one of the ⅜-inch cocks with a short piece of hose, and the air should be pumped into it until the upper tank rises to its highest level.

The pressure in this form of air holder must be regulated by weights, and to secure 1 pound of pressure it is necessary to place weights equal to 1 pound for every inch in area contained in the opening in the upper tank. Two drop handles, such as are used on heavy milk cans, should be riveted and soldered on the sides of the tank to facilitate moving it about.

Air Holder No. 3.

Fig. 12 is a cut of a bellows with a contained air holder. It is not practical to try to make this article, as it can be purchased from any plumbing supply house and is not expensive. It is used principally by dentists, but it is also used in laboratories to supply air to the compound blow pipe. It consists of a small bellows held from the floor on iron legs, with a spring inside the bellows to hold them open, and has a rubber bag fastened to the under side to hold a small supply of air. The rubber bag is incased in a string net to prevent it from becoming inflated too much and bursting. This bag serves to equalize the pressure. The size known as No. 10 A will supply 75 cubic feet per hour at a pressure of 1½ pounds to the square inch, which is sufficient for lead as heavy as 24 pounds. For the light weight leads the pressure can be reduced by pumping lightly and not filling the bag more than half full.

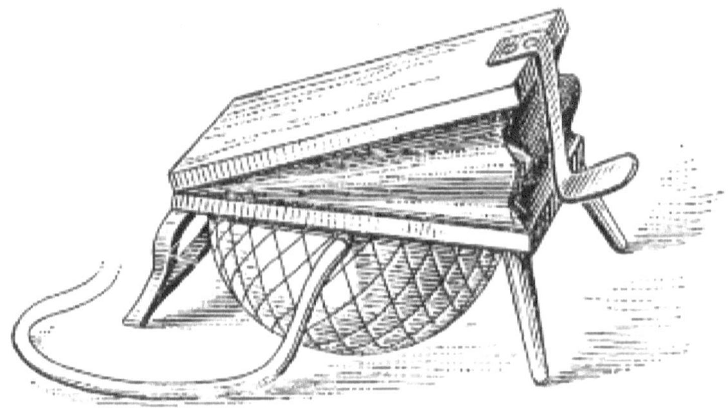

FIG. 12.—AIR HOLDER NO. 3, COMBINED WITH BELLOWS.

Any of the three described air blast arrangements will answer the purpose, so it is immaterial which is used, and it is left to the discretion of the beginner to obtain whichever is the most convenient.

The Blow Pipe.

Next comes the blow pipe. The only practical compound blow pipe on the market is shown in Fig. 13, and is known as Walmsley's. This is a modification of the Bunsen burner, and consists of a bent blow pipe with the air tube in the center, as shown in Fig. 14. It is a perfect working blow pipe in every respect, and I should advise every one interested in the work to purchase one. For while seams cannot be burned with it in any other position than horizontal, it will be found useful in lengthening traps or lead bends, for which purpose it is well adapted and can be put into instant use, thereby saving its cost many times over in wiping solders.

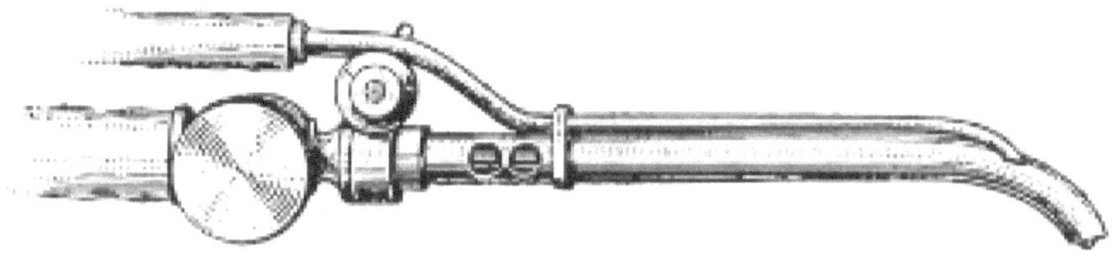

FIG. 13.—THE WALMSLEY COMPOUND BLOW PIPE.

Burning with Illuminating Gas.

With illuminating gas it is only necessary to connect the gas jet to the compound blow pipe with the hose and regulate the supply of gas with the gas cock. The air inlet is then connected to the air holder, or air may be supplied with the mouth, but good results are not obtained with the mouth, as only a good blow pipe solderer can keep up the blast necessary. To burn the seams use the same flux and follow directions given for gasoline gas.

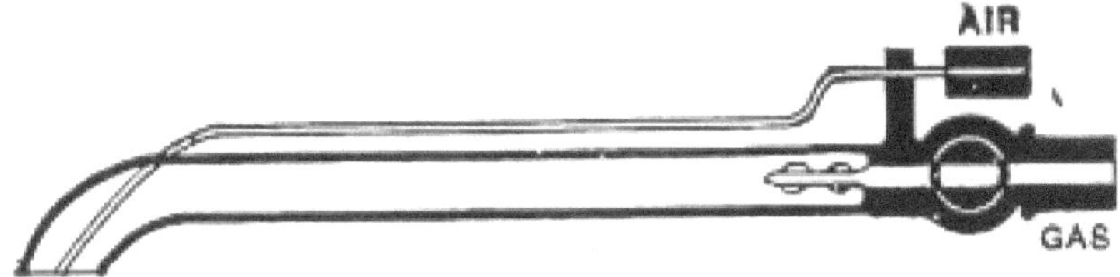

FIG. 14.—SECTIONAL VIEW OF WALMSLEY'S BLOW PIPE.

Making the Gasoline Gas for Burning the Generator.

With a piece of ¼-inch hose connect the top of the can C, Fig. 9, with the air holder D, then connect the spout or gas outlet e of the can to the gas end f of the compound blow pipe. The air outlet g of the compound blow pipe should then be connected to the remaining cock h, in the air holder. If the bellows is used, it will be necessary to connect the air with ¼-inch tee, m, in which three short nipples have previously been screwed.

The apparatus is now ready for use. Gasoline being really a liquid gas, it takes its first opportunity to assume its natural shape. The natural way to convert gasoline into gas is by simple evaporation. So taking advantage of this fact, the action will be thus: By forcing air into and through a body of gasoline sufficient of the gasoline is taken up to form a dense vapor, which will light and burn at the jet, similar to illuminating gas. With the admixture of air in the compound blow pipe, it gives a flame of very intense heat. But, in common with illuminating gas, it is so rich in carbon that it gives an oxidizing flame, and makes it necessary to use a flux, which should be Yager's soldering salts mixed as per the directions on the bottle. If this is difficult to procure, a good substitute can be made by mixing equal parts of powdered borax and sal ammoniac in a little water.

To operate this device the air should be turned on the gasoline and lighted at the jet. The air should then be admitted gradually until the flame is brought to the proper size and condition, indicated by its being blue and pointed. If too much gas is admitted the flame will be yellow and will blacken the work by depositing a coat of soot on it. If too much air is admitted the flame will be ragged and noisy, and the temperature will be too low to heat the metal. The flame is at its best heat when it burns with a pale blue color which does not show any yellow streaks.

Before attempting to burn the generator the beginner should practice on pieces of sheet lead. It is next to impossible to burn seams in any other position than horizontal with this flame, as it rapidly oxidizes the lead, and in spite of all precaution the lead will become unmanageable in upright seams, so that the beginner would waste time in practicing on seams in any other position than horizontal. If directions have been followed in cutting the lead for the generator the seams will occur only in that position.

To burn the generator the seams should be shaved clean, both on the under and upper sides, for a distance of ⅛ inch, making a seam ¼ inch wide, taking care to have the lead seams lie close to each other, for, if they do not, this flame will cause the edges of the lead to spread away from each other and leave a hole that is difficult to patch.

Now apply the flux with a small brush. When the flame is in working order bring it quickly to bear on the end of the seam nearest you to be burned. When it starts to fuse draw the flame as quickly away, always drawing it to one side, and from the upper to the lower sheet. The melted drop will follow the flame and unite with the melted drop on the lower sheet.

It is necessary to have the shave hook near at hand, so that, in case of oxidizing when fusing, the melted drop can be broken up and allowed to flow in place.

With a little practice and patience the generator can be burned all right in this manner. This gas is perfectly safe and can be handled with impunity. This method would, of course, be impracticable to use on a job of any size, but I have used it several times where nothing else could be obtained, and have always had very good success with it.

CHAPTER VI.

CONNECTING THE APPARATUS.

We now assume that the generator is charged and the rest of the apparatus is finished and ready for use, so we will proceed to connect it up ready for a trial.

About 30 feet of ¼-inch heavy rubber tubing should be procured. This hose should be heavy enough to allow of its being pulled around without kinking and shutting off the supply of gas. A piece of this hose 5 feet long should be slipped on the gas cock M on the generator, shown in Fig. 1, and then slipped over the gas inlet tube of the scrubbing cup n. One must be sure that this is connected to the gas inlet tube, which is the tube that dips under the water in the scrubbing cup.

With another 5-foot piece of hose connect the gas outlet of scrubbing cup o to the right hand cock on the mixing fork f. Always connect the gas on the same side so as to avoid confusion of cocks. Then with a 10-foot piece of hose connect the air cock on the air holder p or bellows to the remaining cock on the mixing fork g. An 8-foot piece should be connected from the gas outlet on mixing fork e to the blow pipe i.

These tubes must fit tight to prevent any possible leak of gas, and if they do not they should be tightened on with pieces of wire. The remaining piece of hose can be used to connect the air pump C to the air inlet cock s on the air holder, but if the bellows are used this will not be needed.

Now place in the scrubbing cup a half dozen pieces of blue vitriol, or copperas, as it is commonly called. Then pour in clear water until it flows out of the trap screw z. This screw can be made tight by using for packing a piece of wicking which has been saturated with tallow. After preparing the apparatus as above, refer to the cut of the complete apparatus and compare the connections on the cut with those made from the above directions, to make positive that they are right. If they agree, the apparatus is now ready for use.

Testing the Apparatus.

It is necessary to test the generator for leaks, as a small blow hole may sometimes be left in some of the seams or the cocks or cleaning screws become defective.

To do this, first close the gas cock on the top of the gas chamber and make up the cleaning and charging screws, which must be set on a bed of soft putty. Then fill the acid chamber full of hot water, first measuring the water so as to ascertain just how much solution is required in proportion to the amount of water, as it takes the same quantity at all times. Allow it to stand for a few moments, then mark the water line with a pencil or nail, when it should be left standing for an hour. The water should stay at the mark indicated for an indefinite time. If it sinks during this test it shows that there is a leak in the generator and it must be located and repaired.

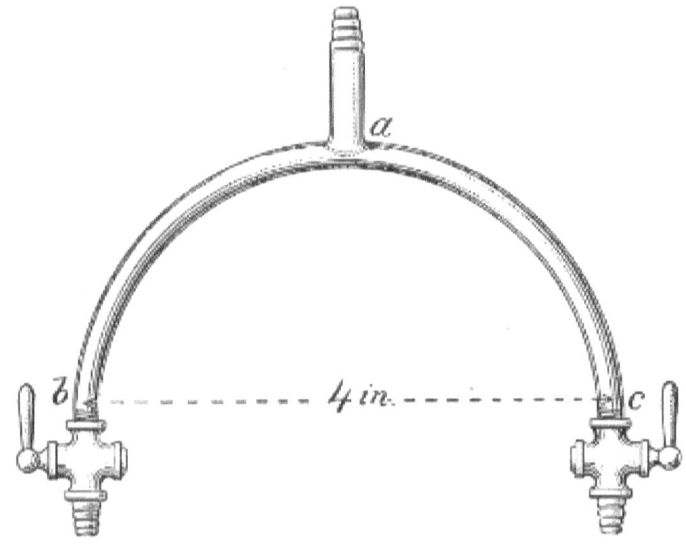

FIG. 15.—MIXING FORK.

To locate the leak the gas cock should be opened and the water allowed to run into the gas chamber. If this does not show the leak, force the water back into the acid chamber, which is done by attaching the air pump to the gas cock. Then taking a piece of soap and making a stiff lather, daub it over the cocks and cleaning and charging screw. When the leak is found the escaping air will cause bubbles to be blown. If the leak does not become apparent after the above process, the side boards of the generator should be taken off and the operation repeated on the seams.

Under no circumstances must the apparatus be left until there is absolutely no doubt as to its being perfectly tight, as a slight leak would be likely to cause a disastrous explosion and injure or probably blind the operator. Flying vitriol is not a very pleasant thing to get in one's eyes.

The apparatus should be frequently tested in this manner: Before drawing off the water it is desirable to learn what amount of gas pressure there will be when the generator is charged, so that the pressure of air and gas can be equalized. The mathematical rule for this is to multiply the head in feet by 0.434, and the result will be the pressure in pounds; or an approximate way of determining the pressure is to allow ½ pound pressure for every foot of head. For example: The hight of liquid in the generator measured from the bottom of the acid supply pipe to the top of the water or acid line, when at its highest level, would be 3 feet. Allowing

½ pound for every foot in hight would give a pressure of 1½ pounds, which is slightly in excess of the mathematical rule, which is 3 × 0.434 = 1.302, or 1 pound 4 ounces, but to be accurate it is well to attach a mercury gauge to the gas cock. Note the hight of the column of mercury. Then attach the gauge to the blast apparatus, and if the floating air holder is used, sufficient weight must be put on the top of air holder to raise the column of mercury to a point not quite as high as is indicated by the generator. These weights can then be weighed and a similar weight made of lead to correspond, which can be kept for permanent use. If the bellows are used, the size specified should be obtained, and the pressure will be all right for this size generator without further trouble. If the air holder indicated by Fig. 8 is used, all that is necessary is to make the hights of the water line in both generator and air holder equal, and the pressure must be the same.

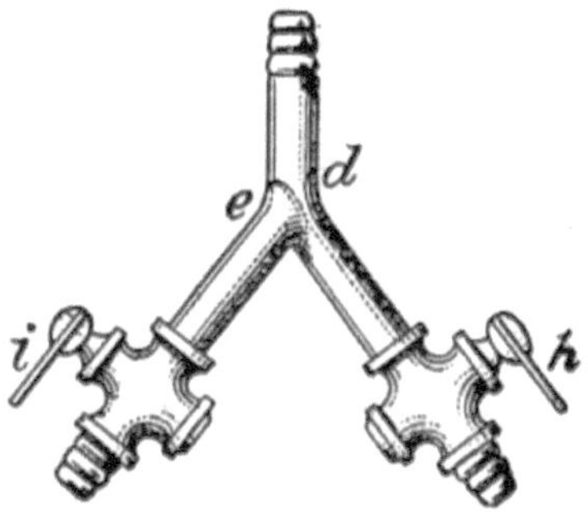

FIG. 16. MIXING FORKS.

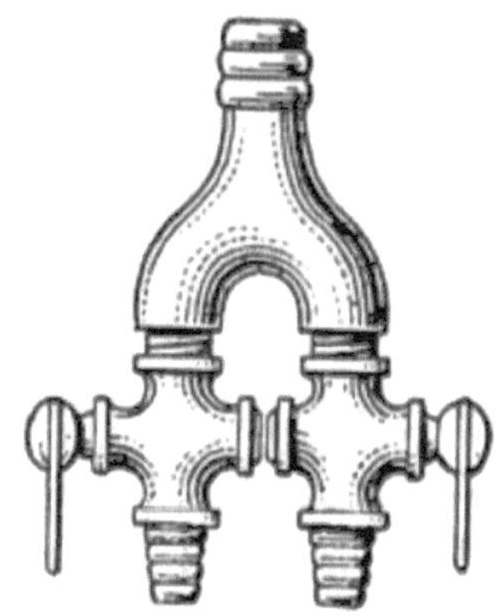

FIG. 17. MIXING FORKS.

The reason that the air pressure should not be heavier than the gas pressure is that if the air were the stronger there would be danger of the air working back into the gas tube and causing an explosion in the tubes; consequently it is well to note this point carefully. Many lead burners will say that the pressure of air is of no consequence, and all that is required is a sufficient supply; but my experience and experiments have convinced me that when the pressures of air and gas are nearly equal the best results are obtained.

The Mixing Fork and Blow Pipe.

The mixing fork and blow pipe can be made in any plumbing shop and should be made of the smallest size pipe available.

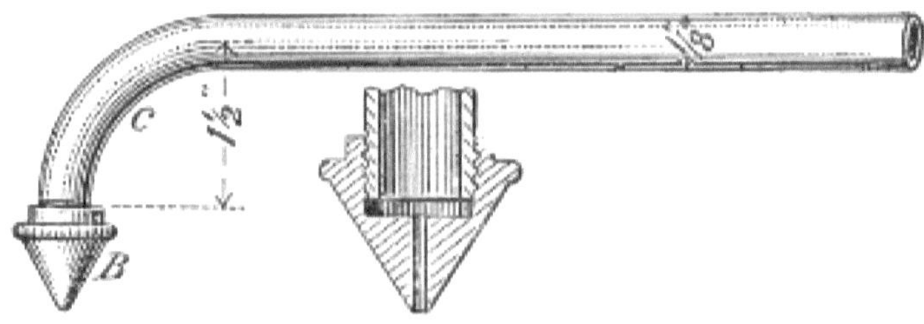

FIG. 18.—BLOW PIPE AND TIP.

To make the mixing fork, purchase two ⅛-inch female hose end gas cocks and 2 feet of ⅛-inch iron pipe size brass tubing. Take a piece of the tubing 12 inches long, cut a regular iron pipe thread on each end, then bend it over a mandrel stake or a piece of 4-inch soil pipe into a half circle, as shown in Fig. 15, so that the ends will come about 4 inches apart. In the center of this piece drill a ⅛-inch hole, *a*. Then cut from the remaining piece of tubing a piece 3 inches long. Solder, or, better yet, have this piece brazed on to the bent piece at *a*, taking care that no solder can run in and partially stop the hole *a*. Then screw the two ⅛-inch gas cocks on the ends *b* and *c*. This will complete the mixing fork; or this fork can be made by bending a piece of pipe at an angle, as shown in Fig. 16; then cut another piece equal in length to the bent piece from the angle *e* to the end. One end of this piece must be filed to fit the piece *d*. A hole can then be drilled at *e*. Threads must be cut on these ends, after which they can be brazed together. Or a good fork can be had by using a special casting. This casting is used for and is known as a beer switch, and can be purchased of any dealer in bar supplies, Fig. 17. The same pattern and size of cocks can be used for this fork as previously described. Neither of these mixing forks has any advantage over the other, but three styles are given, as possibly one may be easier to make than the other. Iron pipe may be used instead of brass if desired.

To make the blow pipe, take the remaining piece of tubing and cut a thread on one end. As the other end slips into the hose, it does not need a thread. The thread end must then be bent at right angles to the tubing, as *c*, Fig. 16. This can be done by boring a hole in a block of hard wood just large enough for the tubing to enter, and 1½ inches deep. Trim off the sharp edge of this hole so as not to kink the pipe in bending. The end of the tube can then be inserted in this hole and bent to the desired shape, as shown. This completes the blow pipes with the exception of the tips, of which you should have three sizes, drilled as follows: One for heavy lead, 3-32; one for medium weight, 2-32, and one for very light sheets, 1-32. These tips are made of small pieces of cast or turned brass, preferably with a milled shoulder, so as to facilitate removing with the fingers. Probably the easiest way to get these tips is to make a pattern out of wood and have several of them cast. They can then be drilled and tapped to any desired size, or they can be cut from a round bar of brass or copper, filed or turned to a point, then drilled and tapped. The dimensions and particulars can be had from B in Fig. 18 without further description being necessary. A common blow pipe, such as is used with the alcohol torch, can be used for practicing on light sheets. But the beginner is advised to procure the blow pipe and a set of tips described in Fig. 18 before attempting to burn any heavy lead.

CHAPTER VII.

CHARGING THE GENERATOR.

After making sure that the generator is perfectly tight we will proceed to charge it. After removing the 4-inch charging screw take 15 pounds of commercial spelter, which has been broken up with a hammer into pieces about 2 inches square, and place this in the gas chamber, distributing it as evenly as possible over the perforated bottom. This is done so that the zinc will expose all the surface possible to the action of the acid, and must be observed in order to obtain the best results. Do not put any pieces of spelter into the generator that are small enough to drop through the perforated bottom, for if they do they will be likely to generate gas, which will give overpressure and blow gas out through the acid chamber. This can do no harm unless close to a light, but it is very annoying to have acid blown all over the generator. The charging and cleaning screws must be screwed up tight. After closing the gas cock on the generator take the quantity of water (less one-seventh) that was found to be necessary when testing the apparatus, and pour this into the acid chamber.

Mark the water line and watch it for a few moments to make sure that everything is tight. Then take of sulphuric acid a quantity equal to one-seventh of the water used, and pour that into the water in the acid chamber. It will diffuse itself through the water and thoroughly mix. Experience has taught me that acid mixed in any proportion stronger than seven parts of water to one part of acid does not act as quickly as when mixed in the proportion mentioned. The reason for this is that the strong acid simply coats the zinc with a deposit or scum of sulphate of zinc, which is soluble in water, but is not soluble in acid. Therefore, if the acid is diluted with water to the above mentioned proportion the water readily dissolves the sulphate and allows the acid to act freely on the zinc.

This sulphate falls to the bottom of the gas chamber and if allowed to accumulate causes the clogging mentioned later. The beginner will observe from the explanation that the generator cannot be crowded by making the solution strong. It sometimes occurs that the vitriol seems to be stronger than usual, and then again the reverse is also true. Good vitriol should be almost as thick as cutting oil, and will work very quickly. Care must be taken in pouring it into the generator to prevent spattering. This is best avoided by having a quart measure made of lead for this purpose. It should also be borne in mind that the *acid should always be added to the water*, never the water to the acid, as this mixture always generates heat, and the result would be similar to adding water to hot lead.

Automatic Action of the Generator.

The generator works best while hot. The gas cock on the generator should now be opened and the mixture allowed to flow into the gas chamber until it spurts out of the gas cock, which must then be closed. By this action all the air in the gas chamber is expelled, leaving it free to generate pure gas at once. This is a sure method of exhausting the air in the gas chamber. The acid then attacks the zinc, causing it to decompose the water and free the hydrogen contained in the acid.

This gas, by reason of its lightness, will rise to the surface of the acid, and as pressure increases it will force the acid back up through the acid supply pipe into the acid chamber, until the acid falls below the perforated bottom. When the acid and zinc cease to come in contact with each other the generation of gas stops until gas is used, which relieves the pressure; then more acid descends, and as it comes in contact with the zinc more gas is generated, replacing that which has been used. This action makes the generator automatic, unless clogging with sulphate of zinc takes place. This may happen at any time if the apparatus is not cleaned after each day's use.

Cleaning the Generator.

To clean the generator in this case attach the air pump to the gas cock on the generator and force the acid up into the acid chamber by pumping air slowly into the gas chamber until the acid rises to the proper hight in the acid chamber, where it can be held by forcing a long wooden plug into the acid supply pipe. The pumping must cease when the acid rises to the proper level, or the excess pressure of air will work up through the supply pipe and cause a blow of acid.

The charging screw can then be removed and the zinc taken out and washed in hot water. Remove the clean out screw and run one or two pails of hot water through the gas chamber. This will remove the deposits of sulphate paste. The zinc can then be replaced, the screws tightened and the acid released again. Be sure and exhaust the air in the gas chamber, as previously described, by letting the air spurt out of the gas cock before connecting it to the scrubbing cup. Care must be taken not to have any lights near the generator when blowing out this mixture of gas and air, as it is very explosive.

The apparatus will never clog if cleaned after each day's work, which should always be done. The tubes should be removed and hung up over night to dry. The acid, if not spent, can be dipped out of the acid chamber and placed in jugs. The generator can then be carried to a drain and filled with hot water, which should be allowed to flow out through the cleaning screw. This will clean the zinc and wash out all the sulphate deposit. The screws may then be tightened and the apparatus left ready for the next day's use.

Fire Trap and Scrubbing Cup.

One of the most essential parts of a lead burning apparatus is a reliable fire trap and scrubbing cup. This trap reduces to a minimum the danger from explosion caused by neglecting to free the gas from air. Its use as a scrubbing cup is also of infinite value.

The action of the vitriol on the zinc produces a violent ebullition, and a small quantity of the acid is carried in the form of spray from the generator to the tubes, and, unless caught and removed, will frequently get into the blow pipe tip and extinguish the flame, making it necessary to remove the hose and hang it up to drain and dry, which oftentimes causes waste of time and annoyance.

Almost all spelter or zinc contains more or less arsenic in a metallic state. It is also found in sulphuric acid. This arsenic is released from the acid or zinc as they decompose and is carried by the force of the volume of gas to the blow pipe tip, where, owing to it being necessary for the operator to get his eyes close to the flames in order to see the reducing flame, this poisonous gas will be breathed into the lungs and oftentimes cause a fatal illness. This fact has been disputed by many, who say that it is impossible for the unit of lightness—*i. e.*, hydrogen gas—to pick up and carry a heavy metal such as arsenic. Arsenic does not form a chemical combination with hydrogen, having a very slight affinity for it, but is carried to the blow pipe solely by the force of the volume of gas.

To prove the above assertion we will refer to Professor Marsh, who demonstrated the ability of hydrogen to carry arsenic in the following manner: If a solution containing arsenic be added to a solution of sulphuric acid and zinc, the resulting hydrogen will, upon ignition, deposit a ring of metallic arsenic upon any cold surface that the flame be directed upon. (Professor Marsh's experiment.)

It will be seen from the above that it is imperative that the operator use a scrubbing cup and see that it is properly filled with a solution of blue vitriol. The ordinary impurities of hydrogen generated in this manner are sulphur and carbon, which should be removed if possible.

The actual use of the scrubbing cup is to catch the above mentioned spray and precipitate to some extent all other impurities contained in the gas, and produce gas sufficiently pure for lead burning.

Directions for Making the Cup.

To make this cup take a piece of 4-inch lead pipe 7 inches long (an ordinary piece of 4-inch lead soil pipe will do); flange out one end and burn in a flat bottom. Three inches from the bottom, and in the side of this 4-inch pipe, burn in a trap screw, *a*, Fig. 19, a screw taken from an old lead trap being just the thing. This is to regulate the hight of the solution in the cup. Now make a top by taking a piece of lead and raising it about ¾ inch; punch two holes in this top, *b* and *c*, large enough to let a ⅜-inch lead pipe pass through; flange out the top of the cup and fit and burn this top in place. Take two pieces of ⅜-inch lead pipe, one to be 3 inches long and the other to be 10 inches long, and with the dresser draw one end of each to nearly a point, so that the hose can be slipped on tight. The long piece *c* should now be slipped through one of the holes in the top of the cup, holding it ½ inch from the bottom *d* and burning it in. This is the gas inlet and should be marked as such. The short piece is then placed in the remaining hole and burnt in place. The action will be thus: The gas entering the gas inlet pipe is caused to pass through a solution of blue vitriol 2½ inches deep, when the acid is caught and the gas is scrubbed and rendered as nearly pure as possible. It then enters the outlet pipe and is ready for use. If the directions have been followed the cup will resemble the illustration Fig. 17. No trouble will be experienced with this cup.

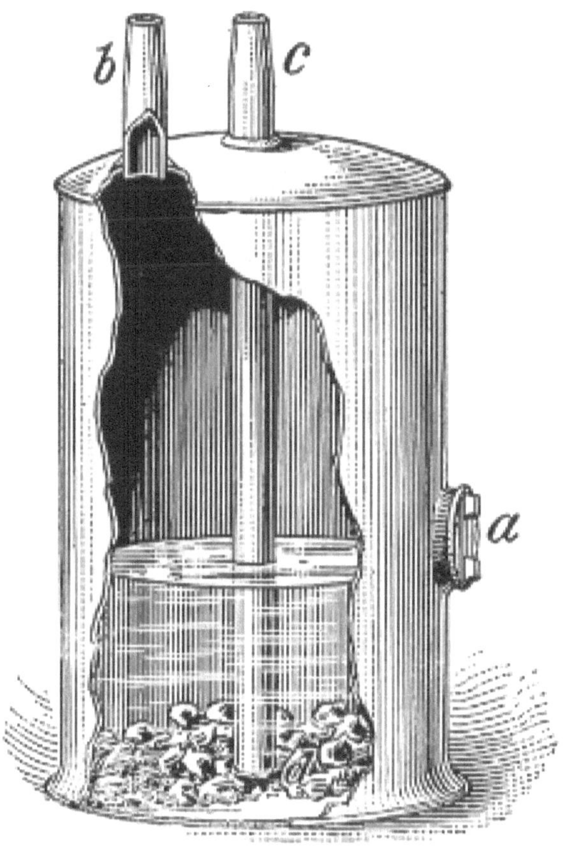

FIG. 19.—FIRE TRAP AND SCRUBBING CUP.

CHAPTER VIII.

THE FLAME AND ITS MANAGEMENT.

Before attempting to light the gas the operator must be sure that all the air is exhausted from the tubes. Otherwise the flame will go back and explode in the tubes or fire trap. To be sure of this the beginner must test the gas. A handy test tube can be made by capping one end of a piece of ½-inch pipe, which should be about 6 inches long. To test the gas, first open wide the gas cock M on the generator, Fig. 1. Then open the gas cock f on the mixing fork and let the gas displace the air in the tubes, which it will do in about one minute. Then invert the test tube, Fig. 20, and hold it over the blow pipe tip for a moment until the gas has displaced the air in the tube. Then quickly place your thumb over the opening of the test tube, which will keep the gas from escaping. Close the gas cock f on the mixing fork, then take the test tube to one side away from the generator, still keeping it inverted, and bring it close to a lighted match or candle. It will light with a pop, and if it is free from air it will burn quietly down in the tube until the gas is exhausted. Continue to test the gas in this manner until it burns as described, when it may be safely lit at the jet without fear of its burning back. This precaution is necessary only after opening the generator for some purpose.

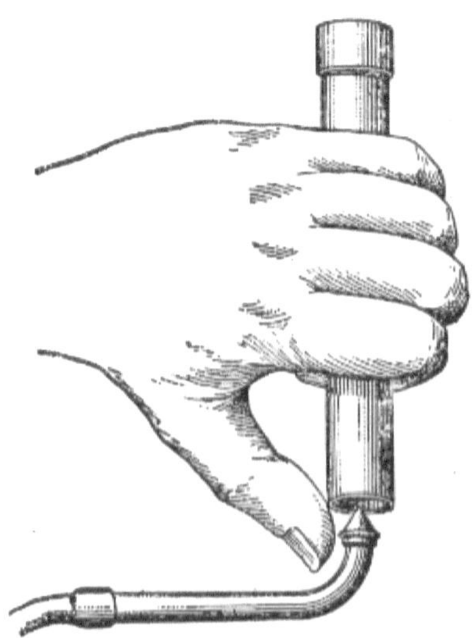

FIG. 20.—METHOD OF TESTING GAS.

Regulating Volume and Pressure.

This generator evolves gas under a greater pressure than can be used on most work, and for this reason the flame will at first be long, noisy and unsteady, as shown in A, Fig. 21, but, as there are two cocks, the volume and pressure can be regulated to the requirements of the work at hand. Now, to note the peculiarities of this flame, we will close the gas cock f on the mixing fork until the flame is about 3 inches long. It will be of a pale reddish color and will burn steadily. The inner flame is not as yet very well defined. Then open the air cock g slowly, and when sufficient air has been admitted the flame will be seen to shoot out suddenly and then shorten to about 1¾ or 2 inches in length. It will be smooth, compact, and will have the appearance of darting rapidly. If the correct quantity of air has been admitted the inner flame, as shown in B, Fig. 21, will then be plainly seen, and its apex, which is the point of greatest heat, will be blue. This inner flame is known as the nonoxidizing flame, and is the flame with which the fusing is done.

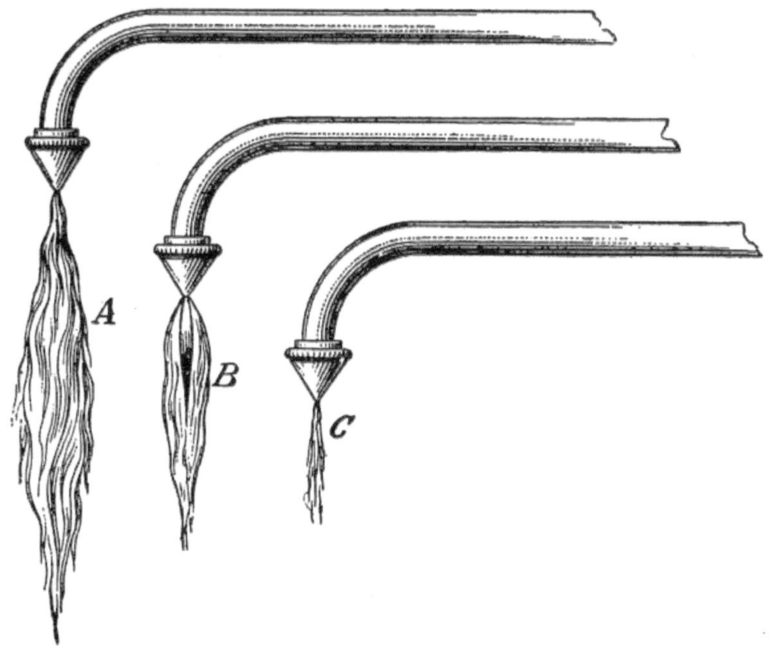

FIG. 21.—FLAMES UNDER DIFFERENT PRESSURES.

The outer flame will change to a bluish color. Its temperature is low, and its effect on the lead is to coat the metal with a heavy blue oxide, under which the lead runs but does not unite. To demonstrate this, bring the point of the inner or non-oxidizing flame to bear on a piece of sheet lead. It will fuse bright and clean and will have a circle of gray oxide around it. Then quickly remove the flame and the spot will remain bright. Now, again bring the flame to bear on the same piece of lead, keeping the point of the inner flame at least ¾ inch away from the lead. It will melt and flow together, but will be covered with a coat of gray oxide and the union will not be perfect. Slowly withdraw the flame, and before the flame is entirely removed the spot will be heavily coated with a thick blue oxide, under which the lead will not unite. C, in Fig. 21, shows the appearance of the flame when too much air has been admitted and it is on the point of going out from lack of gas.

The proper way to use the gas is to open wide the gas cock M on the generator, and do any regulating of the flame with the gas cock *f* on the mixing fork. These cocks should have pieces of heavy wire brazed or soldered lengthwise of the handles, Fig. 16, *h* and *i*, so as to form lever handles. This will allow the gas and air cocks to be closed or opened by gently tapping the levers *h* and *i*, which is the only way that a slight variation can be had, for if you try to regulate them with the finger you will constantly open or close them too much, and the result is that in adding air too much is always admitted, which will blow out the flame, making it necessary to turn off the air and light the jet again, and many times this operation will have to be repeated before the flame is correctly adjusted.

It must be remembered to always turn on and light the gas before admitting any air, and when through with the flame the air must be turned off first, then the gas. If this operation is reversed an explosive mixture of gas and air would form in the tube and would spoil the tube, if nothing worse.

Study the Flame Well.

The beginner should study the flame until perfectly familiar with the color and form of the proper flame. One of the greatest troubles that the beginner will have with the blow pipe is the inability to regulate the flame to the requirements of the work. For instance: A flame that would work nicely on 12-pound sheets would burn holes in 4-pound sheets before you had time to touch the lead with the inner flame. For that reason three different sizes of tips should be used. On a 2-pound sheet the smallest, or 1-32, tip should be used, and the flame before reducing should not be longer than ¾ inch, and when reduced the inner flame can hardly be distinguished, but you can easily tell when it touches the lead by the metal fusing bright. If it is desired to fuse 12-pound sheets the 2-32-inch tip should be substituted, and it would be found necessary to have the jet of gas about 3 inches long, which, when reduced, would be about 2 inches long and would show the inner flame very distinctly.

The only way to determine the size of the flame necessary is by experimenting with it. It will also come with experience. The flame should be reduced to a size that will not melt the lead as soon as it touches it. Rather, it should be in such condition that the lead would have to be heated first and let the fusing come gradually. In that way it can be determined just what sized drop is required, and also plenty of time is allowed to place it just where it is wanted—particularly on upright seams and *imperatively* on inverted seams.

It is not necessary to be so particular on horizontal seams, as on seams in that position you are assisted by gravity. The lead drop that is melted from the upper lap cannot do otherwise than unite with the under lap. It must be remembered that in starting a seam you have cold lead to fuse, and after the first drop is started the lead in its vicinity will be heated almost to the melting point, and you will probably be surprised to see the lead run at the approach of the flame for the next application.

Do Not Hurry.

The point to be taught here is that you must not attempt to hurry this work or holes will surely be burned in the sheets, which oftentimes makes difficult work to patch. The old adage, "haste makes waste," can well be applied to lead burning. Sufficient time must be allowed for one drop to set before attempting to place the next drop. Time spent on practicing at the bench is time well spent, as many little details that cannot be brought to the beginner's attention here will be learned in that way and stored in his mind for future application.

CHAPTER IX.

THE DIFFERENT KINDS OF SEAMS.

There are two kinds of seams proper, viz.: The butt seam and the lap seam. The butt seam is used principally for joining horizontal waste pipes and in lengthening traps, or for any purpose where it is desired not to have the point of junction show. This form of seam can be burned clear through—that is, the lead can be heated until fusion takes place nearly through the entire sheet. It is generally necessary to add lead to the seam if it is desired to make the seam as strong as the sheet it joins, unless the article to be burned is of such a size as to be possible to allow of its being burned on both sides, which makes the strongest of seams. The lead for the butt seams is prepared by rasping the edges of the lead sheet to be joined straight and true, Fig. 22, so that when the edges of the lead are brought together they will fit close its entire length. The edges are then shaved for a distance of ⅛ inch each side of the edge, making a seam ¼ inch wide. On stock heavier than 12-pound sheets the edge should be shaved off, making a deep V-shaped groove, and the seams must be made by adding lead. This allows the fusion to take place nearly through the sheet. The butt seam is the simplest form to burn, no matter in what position it is placed.

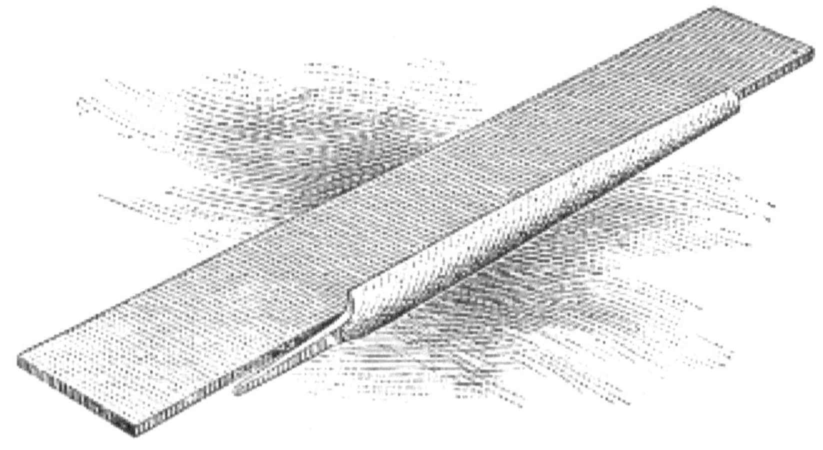

FIG. 22.—RASPING THE EDGES OF THE LEAD SHEET STRAIGHT AND TRUE.

The lap seam is the seam commonly used, and as between the butt seam and the lap seam the latter is generally to be preferred. As it is not necessary to cut and trim the edges true, it dispenses with any additions of lead, except at rare intervals; it leaves the left hand free to handle the shave hook, and the lap can be dressed to fit any uneven spots. It also makes the next best seam to through fusing. By lap seaming a tank can be lined in about half the time required to butt seam the same article, which is an important item to the customer.

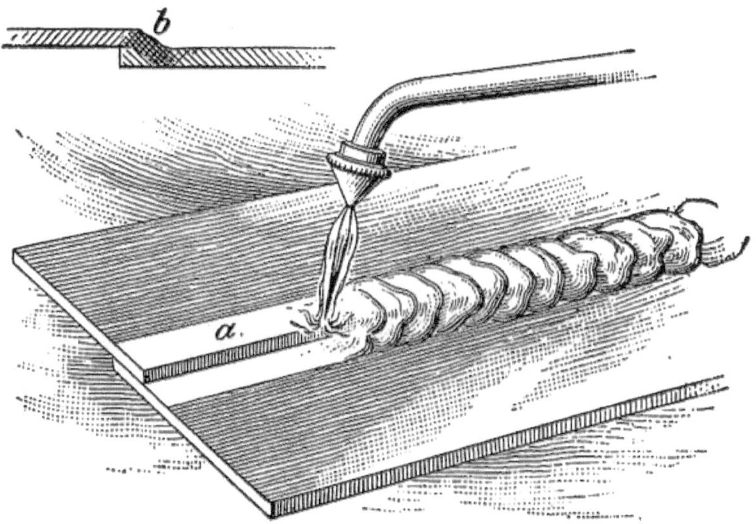

FIG. 23.—BURNING A LAP SEAM.

The lead for this form of seam is prepared, as its name indicates, by lapping one sheet ½ to ¾ inch over the other sheet. The under edges are to be shaved clean, as also the upper edge. The lead required to make the seam is melted from the upper lap and is fused on the lower sheet. There is no reason why the lead at the point of juncture cannot be made as thick as the original lead. This is the point aimed at in practicing, and the only accurate way to determine the relative strength of the seams is to cut squarely across a finished seam, then bend the beam slightly. The thickness can then be noted. A cross section of a perfect lap seam is shown at *a* in Fig. 23. The beginner should practice the different seams until the thickness of the joint can be told by the looks of the lead. A few days' diligent practice at the bench will soon train the eye to note any imperfection that may arise.

The different seams will be taken up serially. A description of how the seams are prepared and the several positions of the blow pipe, as well as the little difficulties that may arise, is the extent of the instruction that can be given. The rest must come with practice and the application of a little common sense. There is no royal road to this business; but practice, and practice hard, is the only way to satisfactorily master the blow pipe and flame, and in practicing remember that all this work has been done before, and can be easily done again, *and by you*. Do not get discouraged by failure to make a perfect seam at the first application, but stick to it for a short time and it will be found to be a most fascinating pastime, for which the persistent student will eventually be well repaid.

Flat Butt Seam.

For practicing I would recommend the beginner to use pieces of sheet lead about 12 inches long, as strips of that length are much easier to prepare. The edges are straightened with a fine rasp which is held lengthwise of and parallel to the edge to be trued, in the manner shown in Fig. 22. The rasp must be used lightly, or it will be apt to tear the lead and so leave it in worse condition than before using it. The edge should then be gone over with the shave hook and cleaned. Then shave the top surface a distance of ⅛ inch each way from the edge, which will make a seam ¼ inch wide when finished. Then butt the edges together and secure the sheets firmly to a board with a few tacks. The extra lead that is necessary to add to make a butt joint full must be obtained from a strip of lead, which should be about ⅛ inch square and *shaved clean.*

After regulating the flame to the proper size and shape the burning should be begun at the end of the seam nearest the operator. With the point of the inner flame melt off a drop from the lead strip and have it fall squarely on the seam just slightly in advance of the point of fusion. Follow it up with the flame, placing the point of the inner flame directly over the edges of the seam, which is almost under the lead drop. As soon as fusion commences on the lead seam the melted drop will flow to the bright spot and immediately unite with it. The flame must then be quickly removed and the drop be allowed to set.

In order to avoid any misunderstanding regarding the time required for the lead drop to set I would say that the drop will cool immediately upon the flame being removed from contact with it. It is not necessary to wait for any specified time, but if the flame is allowed to play constantly on the sheet it is apt to get over-heated, and when in that condition it takes very little heat to set the lead running like water. To avoid this the flame should be lifted clear of the seam for an instant after each drop has been fused into place.

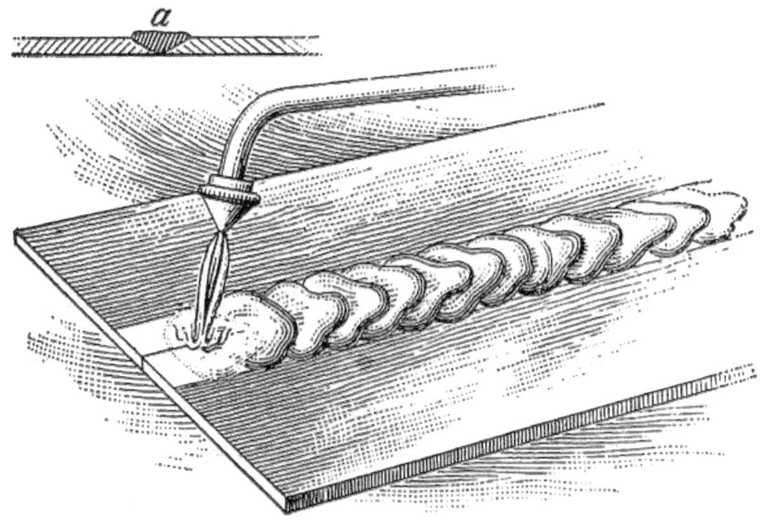

FIG. 24.—BURNING A FLAT BUTT SEAM.

These remarks apply to all seams that are made by the blow pipe process and should be noted, as this particular point will not be referred to again. Now melt off another drop and let it fall as before, only it should lap on the previous drop about one-half its diameter. Secure it to the seam as before. This operation should be repeated until the seam is completed, and if the seam is correctly done a section will appear as *a* in Fig. 24. This form of flat seam should be practiced until perfectly familiar with the blow pipe flame and until the beginner can approach the lead with the flame without burning holes through it, which will probably be the first thing to happen.

Upright Butt Seam.

The upright butt seam is seldom used on large work, as it is a difficult matter to make an upright butt seam that will stand the test, as, if a finished seam is cut into short pieces, an examination of the severed ends will show many weak places that were previously thought to be very strong. The reason of this is that the heat necessary to fuse through the lead will cause the lead to run from the seam and leave a hole.

The sheets for practice are prepared as described for flat butt seams, and must be securely tacked to a board which can be supported in an upright position. The burning is begun at the bottom of the seam. The flame must be shortened considerably, as the fusing must take place somewhat slower than in flat seams, as in upright or inverted seams the attraction of gravity remains to be overcome, and the operator must have plenty of time between the commencement of brightening and the actual fusing to drive the melting drop to the exact position desired.

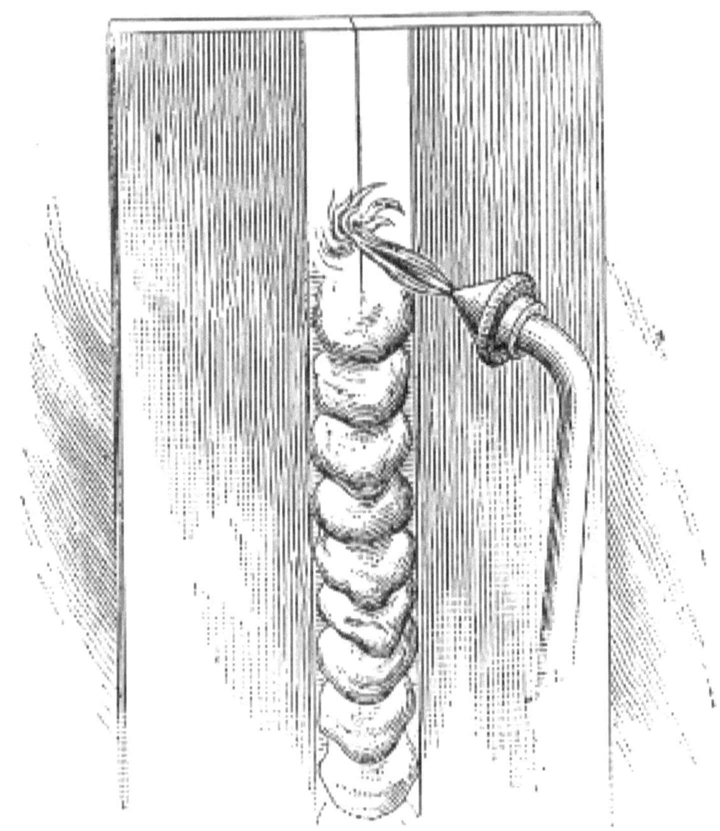

FIG. 25.—BURNING AN UPRIGHT BUTT SEAM.

The blow pipe is held so that the flame strikes the seam squarely and at about a right angle with the sheet, as shown in Fig. 25. When fusion starts the flame should be drawn quickly to one side, and if the lead is at the proper temperature the melted drop will follow the point of flame, and as it comes in contact with the adjoining edge it will properly unite. It is not necessary to add lead to these seams oftener than at intervals of 5 or 6 inches, or as often as the lead shows signs of weakening, when it may be added by holding the lead strip against the lead sheet and slightly above the flame. The melted drop will unite with the sheet and can then be driven to any desired position. This seam will show the characteristic beads, but they will lie nearly level with the lead sheets, and if a scratch cloth be rubbed over the seam all traces of the position of the seam will be removed.

To make a really strong seam it must be gone over with the flame at least twice, as after fusion of the edges takes place the flame can be used quite strong without fear of the lead running from the seam. Do not leave this seam until you are satisfied that it is nearly perfect. It is good practice, and every hour spent only makes the mastery of the next seam come so much more quickly.

Horizontal Butt Seam.

This form of seam cannot be used to any advantage on general work, but, like seams in other positions, it cannot always be avoided. The practice sheets are prepared and tacked securely to the board, as previously described, and are then placed in the position shown in Fig. 26. The position of the blow pipe is as shown at *a*. The flame should strike the sheet nearly square. The edge of the upper sheet should be heated first, and as it brightens the flame should be directed onto the edge of the lower sheet. If properly done, fusion will at once take place.

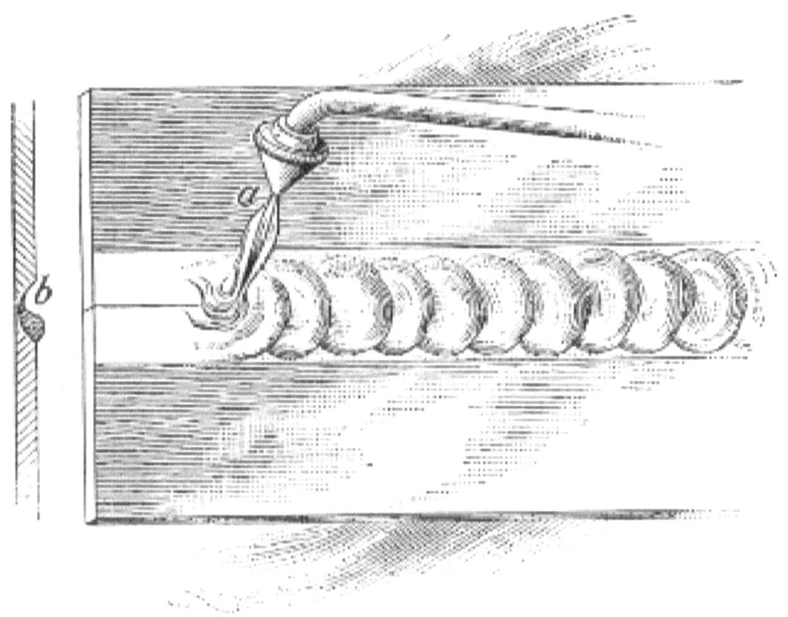

FIG. 26.—BURNING A HORIZONTAL BUTT SEAM.

The object sought is to get a light fusion between the two sheets before attempting to burn the lead clear through the seam. If this is not done, the lead will run from the upper sheet and cause holes, or at least will seriously weaken the upper sheet, as shown in cross section at *b*. After fusion is once obtained it is a simple matter to go over the seam a second time, which can then be fused clear through without much danger of burning holes through the sheet. Lead can be added in the same manner as in upright seams if necessary.

Inverted Butt Seam.

This seam is used extensively in joining waste pipes which conduct the acid from tanks to the drain. These pipes are usually in a horizontal position and the seams must be burned in place. The most difficult part of the seam is in starting it. When fusion has once taken place the balance of the seam is easy. The seam is prepared the same as described for other butt seams. Care must be taken to have the edges butt close. The board can then be supported in the required position by any convenient device.

The blow pipe flame must be made as short as possible and still melt the lead. The point of the inner flame is then placed squarely on the seam. Both edges must be heated at once. If the edges begin to brighten and do not show an inclination to fuse, the flame should be drawn quickly to one side, and the melted drop will follow the point of flame and unite with the adjoining edge. This seam, in common with the other butt seams, should be gone over the second time to assure a perfect seam. It is difficult work to add lead to the flat inverted seam. When necessary to do so, however, it can be added by burning the end of the lead strip to the seam. The strip is then melted off, leaving a drop of lead affixed to the seam, which can then be drawn to the required spot with the flame.

The characteristic inverted seam shows pits upon examination of the reverse side of the sheets. These are caused by overheating. The operator will often be surprised at the inverted butt seam showing a remarkable fullness. This is accounted for upon the examination above referred to. The lead, upon the application of the heat, runs from the upper or back side of the sheet and forms a very full seam. For that reason the inverted butt seams always appear stronger than they really are. See inverted lap seam, Fig. 27.

Lap Seams.

The lap seams are the seams commonly used on all classes of work. When the beginner becomes proficient with the blow pipe no trouble will be experienced in making lap seams that will show when cut a joint equal in thickness to the sheets that are joined. The lead sheets for the flat lap seam are prepared by shaving clean the exposed edge; also, shave the sheets where they touch each other. The upper edges can then be shaved for a distance of ⅛ inch each side of the lap, which will make the finished seam ¾ inch wide, as shown at *a* in Fig. 23. The sheets should be lapped ½ to ¾ inch, according to the weight of the stock. It is very evident that light weights would not require as large a lap as would heavier sheets, as the object of lapping the sheets is to leave the sheets practically as one piece, and the lead, to accomplish this object, is to be melted from the upper sheet.

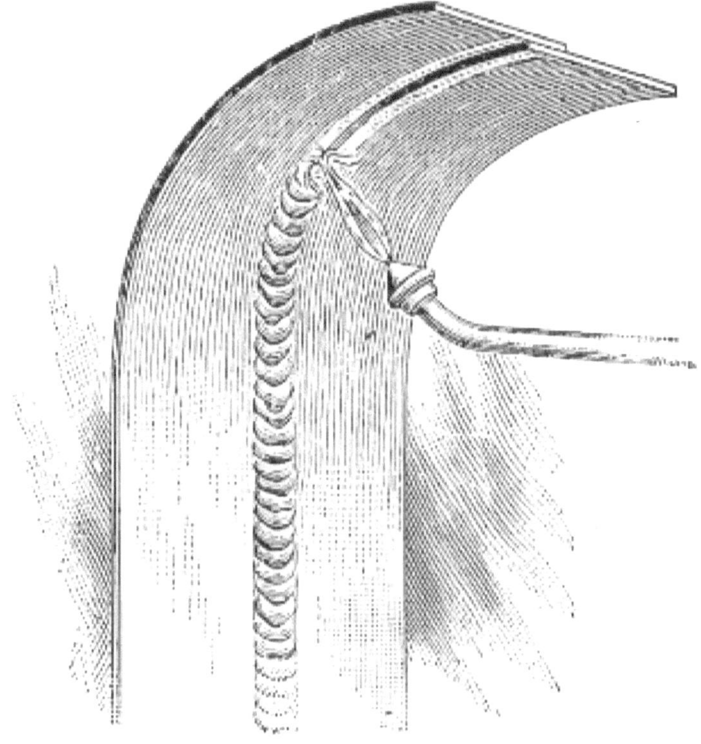

FIG. 27.—BURNING AN INVERTED LAP SEAM.

From the foregoing it will be seen why a 12-pound sheet requires a ½-inch lap, while a 24-pound sheet would require a ¾-inch lap. The flame, when regulated to the work, is brought to bear squarely on the edge of the upper sheet, slanting slightly in the direction of the lower sheet, as shown. When the edge has brightened almost to the fusing point the blow pipe should be drawn quickly to one side and from the upper sheet to the lower sheet. If the metal is sufficiently hot the melted drop will follow the point of the flame and instantly fuse with the lower sheet, and if properly done the seam will resemble *b* in Fig. 23. This process is repeated, advancing about ⅛ to ¼ inch each time. Do not attempt to fuse a large surface at a time. Experts cannot do such a thing satisfactorily, so why should a beginner try to? Rather, try to fuse small surfaces quickly and strongly, as better work and more of it can be accomplished in that manner.

Horizontal Lap Seams.

This seam is prepared precisely as described for flat lap seams. The strips can be fastened to a board with a few tacks. The strips can then be supported in the position shown in Fig. 28. The burning is commenced, as before, at the side nearest the operator. The flame must be made as short as is consistent with the weight of the stock. It will be found to the beginner's advantage to have fusion take place slowly. The point of the inner flame is brought to bear on the outer edge of the lapped sheet and at an angle of 45 degrees. Both sheets should begin to brighten at about the same time. The melted drop must be driven against the back sheet by the force of the jet of flame, and if the sheets are clean fusion will take place quickly.

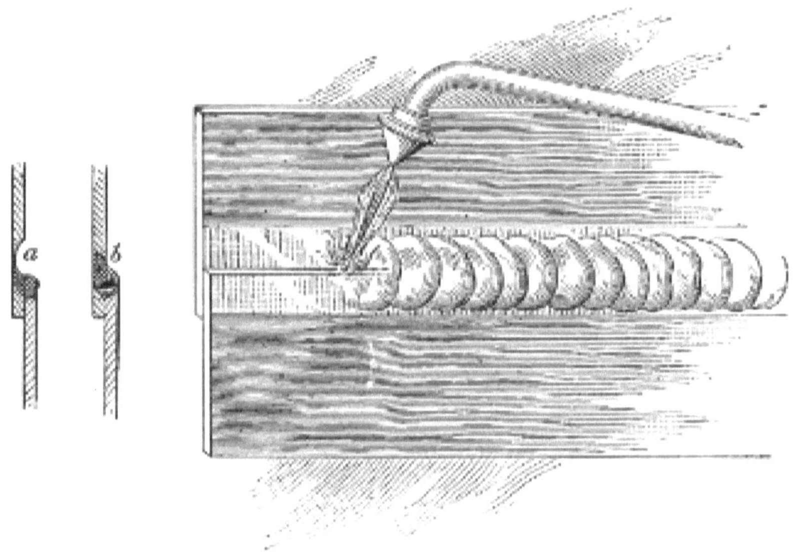

FIG. 28.—BURNING A HORIZONTAL LAP SEAM.

The drops or beads of lead will appear very small on this form of seam, owing to that great obstacle, gravity, which causes the drop when melted to flow downward and so swell the seam. The drops, in common with other forms of lap seams, should be made short, letting each drop overlap the previous drop as much as possible. Great care must be taken not to weaken the seam, as shown at *a*. The beginner should strive to get the seams so that when cut into small sections each section will resemble the result shown at *b*.

Upright Lap Seams.

Prepare the sheets as for flat lap seams, fastening the sheets securely to a board, as previously described. The burning should be begun at the lowest point of the seam. After regulating the flame, the point of the inner flame is applied to the edge of the outer sheet slightly above the point decided upon as the starting point, and at an angle of about 30 degrees, as shown at *a* in Fig. 29. As the drop begins to melt it will have a tendency to flow downward. By a quick turn of the wrist the flame must then be directed against the back sheet and slightly under the melting drop.

The under sheet should brighten at once, and the force of the flame, being partially directed against the melted drop, tends to force it against the bright spot on the back sheet, with which it instantly unites. The flame must then be withdrawn for an instant, to give the fused drop time to set. The operation must be repeated until the seam is finished. Using ordinary language, it may be said that the drop is cut from the upper sheet, carried slightly downward and then stuck against the back sheet by the force of the flame.

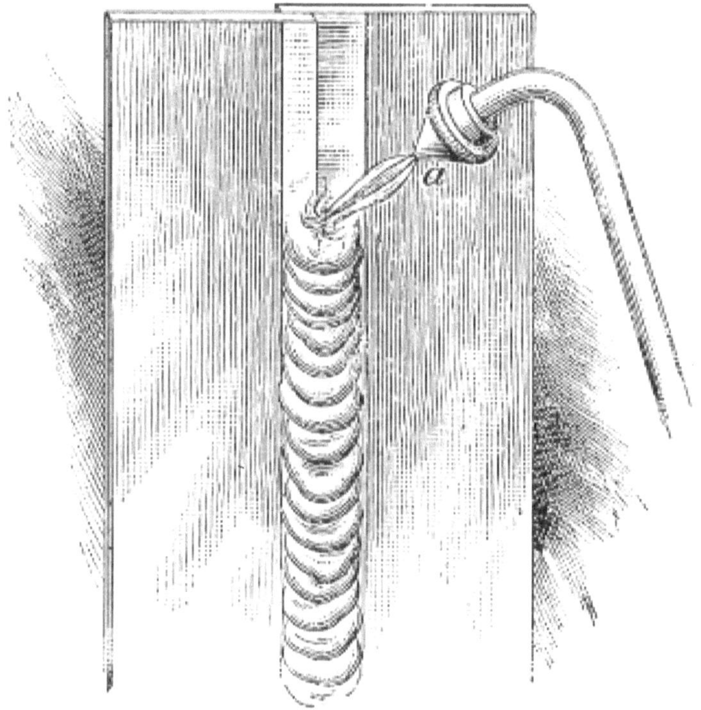

FIG. 29.—BURNING AN UPRIGHT LAP SEAM.

This seam is the one most used, and the beginner should practice it diligently. After mastering it in the position shown in the cut, the board should be fastened to the floor and the beginner should practice burning the upright seam from above the work. This position occurs many times in lining tanks, and the beginner who conquers the upright seam in that position can consider himself sufficiently proficient to attend to any job of lead burning that may arise. The beads of lead will appear more compact and regular than in the flat seam, and if properly done will upon cutting the sample show a very strong joint.

Inverted Lap Seam.

This seam should be attempted only after becoming very proficient with the blow pipe and flame, after which it becomes as easy to burn as in any other position. In order to get the range of the seam the sheets should be arranged in the position shown in Fig. 27. The burning is begun on the upright seam, and continued up and over the curved portion and on to the inverted seam. The graduation from the upright seam to the inverted seam is simple and gradual, and is hardly noticeable.

After accomplishing the inverted seam in this manner, strips of lead should be prepared and fastened to the board as described for upright seams. The board should be supported in an inverted position at a convenient hight over the operator's head. The flame should be shortened as much as possible. The burning may be started at any convenient point and continue in each direction. The point of the inner flame is applied to the seam at a slight angle, as *a*. The object is to obtain a fusion between the back sheet and the upper edge of the lap. When this is accomplished fusion proceeds easily.

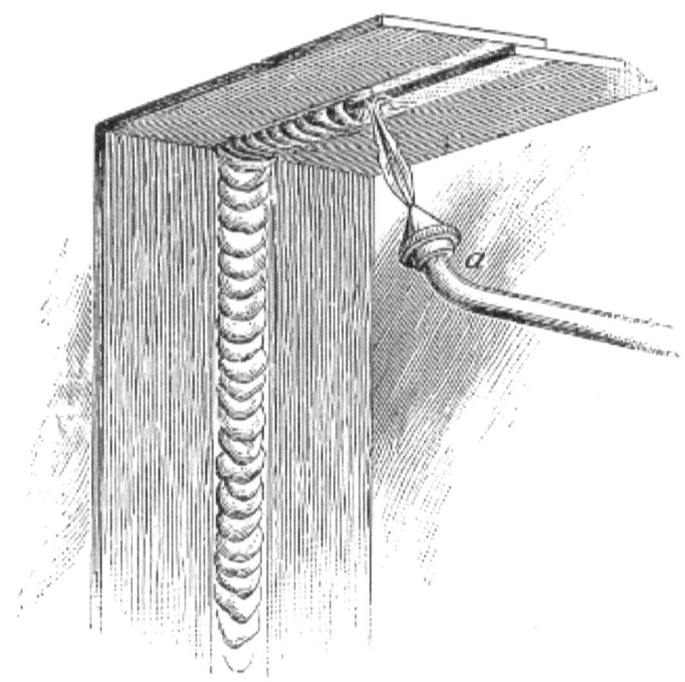

FIG. 30.—BURNING AN INVERTED CORNER SEAM.

The hardest part of this seam is in starting it, and when once started, with a little patience and care, the balance of the seam can be fused without any trouble. Fig. 30 shows an exercise which the beginner should practice after having conquered Fig. 27, as it teaches the making of an inverted corner seam. Of course, this position seldom occurs in small work, but if the burning of it is once accomplished it will give the operator considerable confidence in his own ability.

CHAPTER X.

PIPE SEAMS.

The Butt Seam on Round Pipe.

Pipes that are placed in a horizontal position are usually butt seamed, as a stronger seam can be made in that manner. This form of seam is also used in lengthening traps, bends, etc. To prepare a round pipe for butt seaming, the ends of the pipe should first be made perfectly round by inserting a drift plug and dressing the lead up close to it. The ends of the pipe should be rasped true and then shaved clean. Also shave the pipe for a distance of ⅛ inch each side of the edge. A piece of stiff writing paper should then be rolled up the size of the pipe and inserted in the ends. This paper will prevent any lead from running into the pipe and leaving rough edges, as these afterward form an obstruction.

The burning should be commenced at the under side of the pipe, Fig. 31, and proceed both ways from the starting point and finish at the top. If the beginner has successfully overcome the difficulties of the seams preceding this he will find no trouble in making a strong and workmanlike seam on this pipe. Pipes are seldom used heavier than the grade known as D for this class of work, and for that reason it is seldom necessary to add lead to these seams. But if a hole should be burned in the pipe on the under side, lead should be added to the top side of the pipe and then made to follow the flame to the desired spot. This will be found a quicker and more certain method than attempting to add lead directly to the hole. A properly burned pipe should show the full thickness of the pipe when cut with a saw.

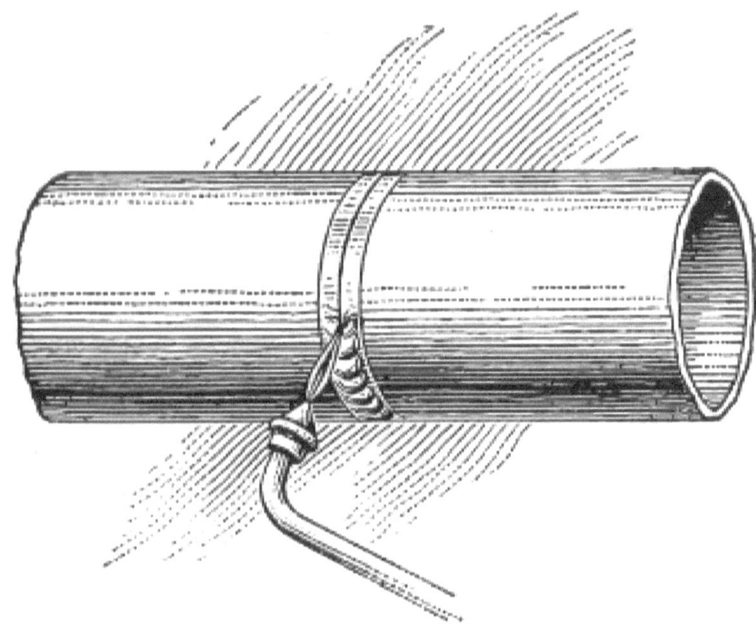

FIG. 31.—BURNING A BUTT SEAM ON ROUND PIPE.

Through Seam on Round Pipe.

Where heavy pipe that is to be used under pressure is to be joined it must be burned through to provide strength, and the ends prepared in the same way as just described, but the ends must also be trimmed off all the way around with a slight bevel reaching from the outside almost to the inside bore of the pipe. The bevel must stop so as to allow a narrow square butt end on each pipe. Then when a piece of paper has been placed on the inside to prevent lead running into the pipe, the two ends when butted will present a V-shaped groove, as shown in Fig. 32, reaching all around the pipe. The burning is commenced at the bottom, as shown in Fig. 31, and the two ends securely united. The groove is then filled by burning on additional lead from a thin cleaned strip until the groove is filled and the pipe made as heavy and strong at this point as anywhere on its entire length.

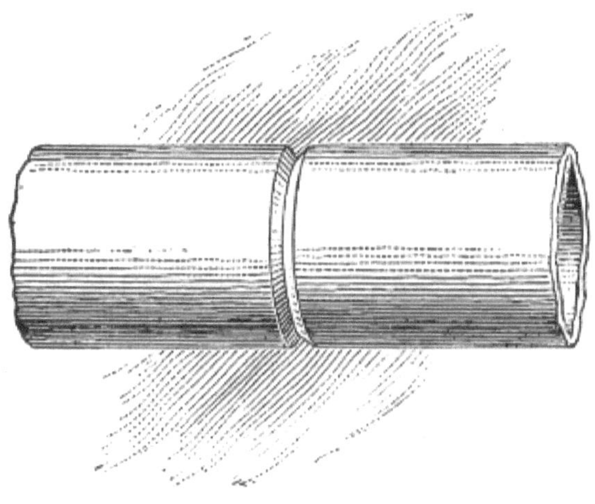

FIG. 32.—JOINT PREPARED FOR THROUGH BURNING.

The Lap Seam on Round Pipe.

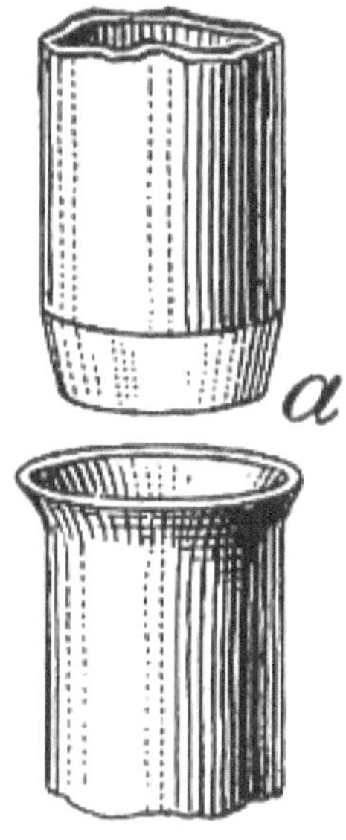

FIG. 33.—PREPARING FOR A LAP SEAM.

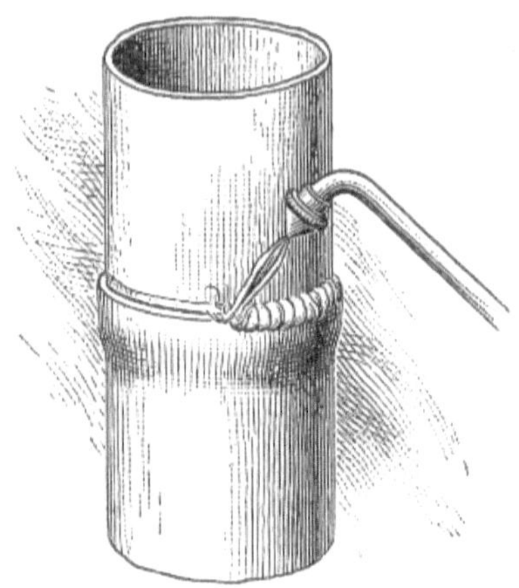

FIG. 34.—BURNING A LAP SEAM ON ROUND PIPE.

This seam is used almost exclusively on pipe in a vertical position, and is similar to the horizontal lap seam. The pipe is prepared by spreading the lower piece of pipe with a drift plug one size larger than the size of the pipe used. The end of the pipe intended to enter this socket is rasped to a bevel edge, as shown at *a*, Fig. 33. This end is then shaved clean, as is also the inside of the socket. The pipe is then placed into the socket, which is then dressed up tight against the inserted pipe, as shown in Fig. 34. The exposed edge is then cleaned and burned, as described for horizontal lap seams.

The Tee Joint on Round Pipe.

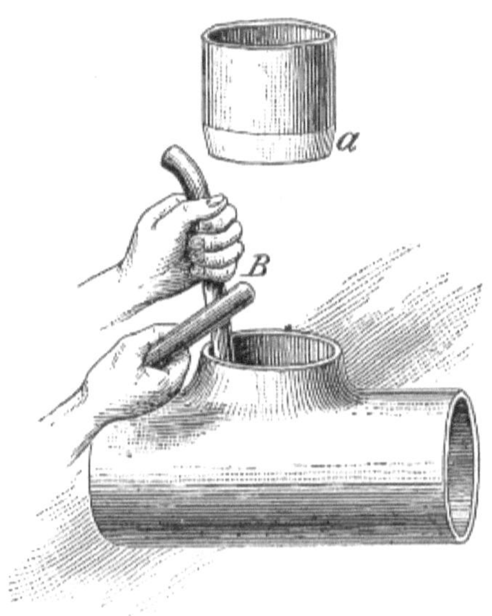

FIG. 35.—MAKING A TEE JOINT ON ROUND PIPE.

With a pair of compasses set the diameter of the pipe that it is desired to insert, and strike a circle on the pipe which is to receive the tee. With a tap borer, or any other device, cut out a circle of lead, leaving about ¼ inch to turn up. Then draw this remaining lead up by means of a bending iron and a heavy piece of iron, such as a chisel, as shown at B in Fig. 35, until the hole is large enough to receive the piece intended for it, the end of which should be beveled with a fine rasp, as shown at *a*. The lead should then be dressed back against the pipe, after which remove the piece and shave clean, and proceed to burn as described for the lap seam on round pipe, and as shown in Fig. 36. Care must be taken in dressing up the lead flange to dress it slowly so as to avoid weakening the lead.

Lining Tanks.

The lining of chemical tanks being the principal work of the chemical plumber, a description of how this work is done will probably be of some use to the beginner. In preparing lead sheets for a tank the sheets should be cut so as to give the most seams on the bottom, because of the greater ease in making them. In large tanks I find it convenient to put the bottom in first, cutting it to make an easy fit, and then the sides are put in. These are cut to allow ¾-inch lap on the bottom.

The lead sheets are laid on the floor, or some other smooth place, which has previously been swept clean, and then dressed out smooth. This can best be done by using the wooden dresser to take out the large wrinkles and then smoothing with a lead flap. This flap is simply a piece of sheet lead about 3 inches wide and 12 inches long, one end of which is drawn into a roll to fit the hand. Then mark the laps and bend them to the desired position. The under side of the lap should be shaved clean, as also the lead under the lap, to facilitate fusion.

FIG. 36.—BURNING IN THE TEE JOINT.

If the tank is over 18 inches high the lead must be fastened to the sides with bullseyes. These are made by countersinking places in the sides of the tank. The lead is then dressed into these holes and it is held in place with large headed brass screws, which are covered by burning over the heads. Lead for the purpose is taken from lead strips. The building up process is resorted to in covering these screw heads.

The lead should be arranged so as to avoid corner seams as much as possible, as it is quite a difficult job to get the proper thickness of lead in such seams. No rule can be given for cutting lead to fit a tank, as tanks are of such a variety of sizes and shapes, and the lead is of so many widths, that the mechanic must study how to cut the stock without waste and have as few seams as possible.

CHAPTER XI.

ACID CHAMBER WORK.

It is not my intention to give an elaborate description of how acids are made or to attempt to describe all of the different fittings employed in that work, because while all plants are similar in construction no two are alike. For that reason I will confine myself to the methods employed in handling lead in large quantities, as the lead used in this work ranges in weight from 18 to 24 pounds to the foot and is therefore very heavy to handle. These chambers are known as condensing chambers, and their use is to catch and condense a mixture of sulphur and steam which is blown into them through a large lead pipe. For that reason they are usually built out of doors, and sometimes have a sort of temporary roof built over them. Consequently in repairing they are easily gotten at, which, by the way, is seldom necessary.

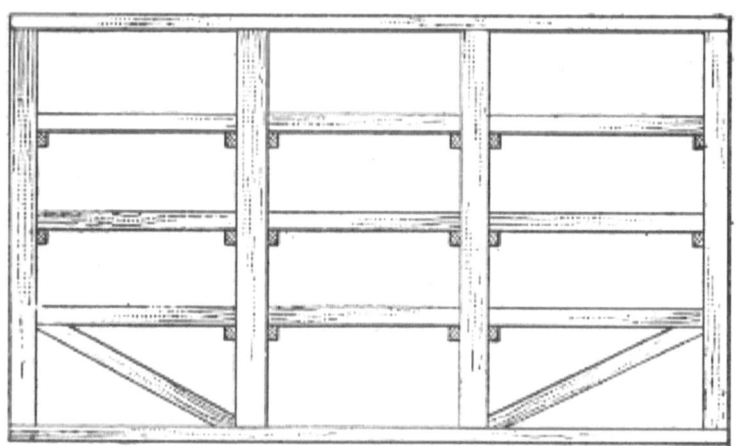

FIG. 37.—METHOD OF FRAMING CHAMBER.

To begin with, the sheet lead should be purchased of such a width as to make as few seams as possible. The bottom of the chamber for this lead to lie upon should be made of 2-inch cypress plank, the same to be tongued and grooved as for floors, and should be planed down, if necessary, so that it will present a perfectly smooth surface for the lead to rest upon, for if there are any uneven spots that is where the lead will eventually crack. The frame work for the sides should also be put in place before the lead work is started, or at least enough of it to prevent dirt and other stuff from bothering the burner. One end of the chamber, however, should be left open, so as to enable the workmen to bring in the lead or other material. The sides should not be closed up, but should be framed, as shown in Fig. 37, so as to allow the lead to be securely fastened to the frame work, which should be made of heavy stock, depending, of course, upon the depth and size of chamber, as they are in all sizes, from 10 feet to 60 feet long and longer.

After seeing that this part of the work is all right, begin to place the bottom in position. This lead should be cut large enough to allow of its being turned up about 2 inches all around for tight tanks. The sides are not burned to the bottoms of some chambers, but the bottom lead is turned up different hights, depending upon how deep it is required to carry the acid in the chamber, which is from 4 to 10 inches or deeper. The studding should be notched out to allow the turned up lead to face with the face of the studding, otherwise there would be a bend in the side lead where it overlaps the sides of the bottom. The flat seams in the bottom should be butted together, so as to give a perfectly smooth surface, which will allow all the acid to be drawn off.

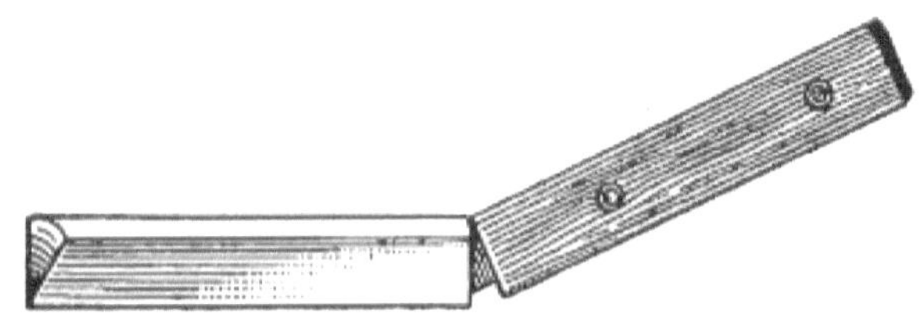

FIG. 38.—CHIPPING KNIFE.

FIG. 39.—(A) STRAP SPLIT AND BENT IN ALTERNATE DIREC-TIONS. (B) BEVEL END OF STRAP.

It is rather a difficult task for some men to cut heavy lead straight. This is easily accomplished by first marking a chalk line on the lead where it is desired to cut it off; then, taking the hammer and chipping knife, as shown in Fig. 38, dip the blade of the knife in water, lay the blade square on the line and strike the back of the blade lightly with the hammer. Mark the sheet the whole length in this manner. Then go over it again and repeat the operation, making sure that the knife is held straight. The blade of the knife must be kept wet or it will stick in the lead and cause it to glance off sideways. After it is cut any uneven spots can be planed off smooth with a small smoothing plane, set so as to take off a very light chip. The lead should now be placed in position and dressed smoothly by using a piece of pine, or other soft board, as a dresser. This must be laid on any uneven spots and then pounded down smooth with a heavy wooden mallet, after which the seams should be shaved and burned at once; or if the seams are short and it is desired to put in enough work one day to keep the burner busy the next, strips of paper 6 inches wide should be pasted over the seams to keep the dust out. Only the edges of the paper should be pasted, so that when ready to burn all that will be necessary is to take hold of one end of the paper and strip it off, leaving the seam clean and free from dust and paste and ready to shave and burn.

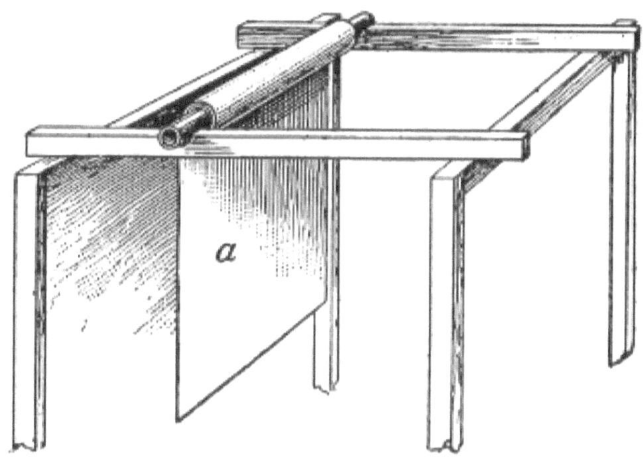

FIG. 40.—ROLL OF LEAD IN POSITION.

After the bottom is finished the sides must be put in, in such a manner as to have as few seams in an upright position as possible, as it saves considerable time to burn them when horizontal. On small chambers or tanks not over 10 feet deep the carpenter should make a staging wide enough to receive two sheets of lead and as long as the tank is deep. The bottom of the chamber should then be covered with boards, so as to prevent damage to the lead. The staging is then brought in and set up on horses, and the sheets of lead are cut off and laid on the staging. The seams are lapped, shaved and burned, after which the lead tacks or straps are cut and burned on, to support the lead when in position.

There are different ways of putting on these straps. For side lead I use strips of the lead itself about 3 inches wide and long enough to lap well onto the studding. My way is to split this strip about ½ inch deep and bend the ends in alternate directions. The edges are then cut off, as shown at A, Fig. 39, after which they are burned in place. These straps should be spaced not more than 15 inches apart, and should be placed in such a manner as to come on the upper side of the studding.

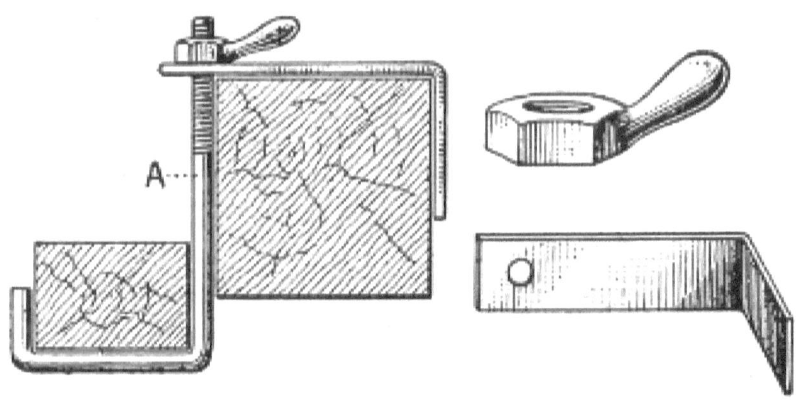

FIG. 41.—CLAMP AND METHOD OF APPLYING.

Another method of putting on these tacks, and one which is most commonly practiced, is to trim the end of the strip of lead as shown at B, Fig. 39. The strip is laid flat on the lead sheet, with the bevel end down, and is then burned onto the sheet in that position, after which it is bent over the studding and nailed. The exponents of this method claim that a better job is done in that manner, as there is always a lifting pull on the strap. I claim for the first method that there is more strength in the lead seam, and that as the edge of the studding comes directly under the strap it acts as a sort of shelf for the strap and thereby becomes a strong brace. But it is probably only a matter of habit, as they hold all right either way.

Now, after having the seams burned and the straps in place, the lead must be put in position. This can be accomplished by any arrangement of block and tackles, but if the chamber be very large it will be found to be a saving of time and labor to rig up a derrick. This is not such an expensive thing to do, as a carpenter is always on hand and most likely all the material needed is already on the ground. This derrick should be constructed with a swinging boom, so that it can be raised, lowered or swung into any desired position.

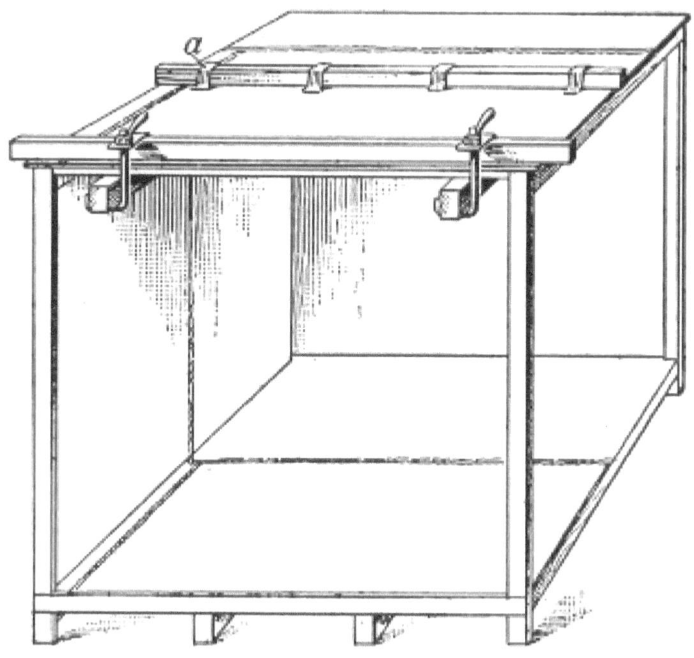

FIG. 42.—SHOWING STAGING IN POSITION.

Now to raise the side lead into position: The derrick is hooked onto the hook or rope that is on the upper end of the staging. It can then be easily raised in position. If the tank be very deep, or if it should be too narrow to follow this method, the sheet lead should be rolled up on a piece of 2, 3 or 4 inch iron pipe, depending upon the weight of the lead. This pipe should be long enough to project at least 6 inches from both ends of the roll. Two timbers, long enough to cross the frame work, should be obtained. About 18 inches from one end of each timber a notch should be cut to prevent the pipe from rolling. These timbers must now be placed across the frame work just over the place that is intended for the lead. The whole roll can now be raised with the derrick and the ends of the pipe placed in the notches. The lead can then be pulled down, similar to pulling down a window shade, after which the tacks can be burned on in place. This is shown at *a*, Fig. 40. Or if there be room enough the piece of lead can be cut from the roll, dressed smooth and have the tacks burned on while on the floor. The upper end of the lead can then be rolled over and nailed to a piece of timber 2 × 6 inches or heavier, and the derrick hooked onto this and raised in position. This is the easiest method where there is room to do it. These are a few of the methods used, but there are numerous other ways.

To place the top lead in position requires a staging, which can be built as follows: Enough hooks should be made to properly support the staging, shown at A, Fig. 41. Two timbers should be laid across the top of the chamber, far enough apart to allow two strips of lead to be placed in position at once. The hooks are now hooked over these timbers, while two pieces of 3 × 3 or 4 × 4 are placed in the other end of the hook. Planks are now laid over these timbers and the screws set up until the tops of the planks come just level with the top of the lead—not higher, or else they will prevent the joist from being placed in position.

The lead can now be cut off on the ground and hoisted up to the top, where it becomes an easy matter to place it in position. The lead tacks can now also be cut and burned on. They should be cut sufficiently long to allow them to lap over the top of the joist, as shown at *a*, Fig. 42, where they should be nailed with large headed nails. It will be noticed that the tacks are doubled up on the top lead and that they are not set opposite each other. The joist can now be set and the tacks nailed on, after which ropes can be tied onto the projecting ends of the 4 × 4 timbers and the whole staging be lowered to the floor at once. This operation can be repeated until the whole top is on.

FIG. 43.—LEAD HEADED NAIL.

It will be necessary to leave small holes between the lead seams at intervals for the hooks to pass through. However, these can be burned over at any time, and where the ends of the top should overlap the end of the chamber the lead can be left turned up until the staging is removed, after which it can be turned over and burned. The hooks are made of ⅝ round iron and have a long thread cut on one end, so as to allow for adjustment. The details are shown in Fig. 41. There are also numerous fittings used in connection with these condensing chambers, but they are all easily made and are too simple to take up space here in explanation. Should it be necessary to use nails for any purpose on the inside of the chamber, the heads should be dipped into a pot of melted lead that has not quite set until the adhering ball of lead is about ½ inch in diameter, as shown in Fig. 43. These nails can be driven in place and the lead burned to the sheet lead, which will prevent corrosion.

CHAPTER XII.

SPECIAL HYDROGEN APPARATUS AND BURNER.

The articles on the universal method of lead burning having been completed, I desire to call attention to a new method and a new generator recently patented and put on the market by the Kirkwood & Herr Hydrogen Machine Company, 3129 South State street, Chicago, Ill. It is called the Kirkwood generator and a general view of it is given in Fig. 44. This generator is a radical departure from the old style generator, as used for the purpose of lead burning, inasmuch as it dispenses with the air blast and consequently with the mixing fork and tubes. The air required to reduce the hydrogen gas to a working condition is obtained by absorbing the air at the mouth of the burner.

The new generator differs also in the amount of pressure used on the gas. With the old style generator, previously described, a pressure of 1½ to 2 pounds is used, whereas the Kirkwood generator is used under a pressure varying from 8 to 30 pounds. At the higher pressure the maker claims the best results are obtained. The generator is made in a size that enables the operator to take it to a job on a street car or train, and that while containing the full charge of acid and zinc, as it weighs when charged about 50 pounds. This is a very important advantage over the old style machine.

Construction of the Generator.

The generator is constructed, so to speak, just the reverse of the old style generator, inasmuch as the lower chamber contains the charge of acid, while the zinc is placed in the upper chamber. The generator shown in the sectional view, Fig. 45, is cylindrical in shape, 9 inches in diameter and 30 inches high. A horizontal partition, to which is burned a pipe long enough to reach to a point about 1 inch above the bottom of the acid chamber, is burned into the cylinder at a point a little above the middle of the cylinder, making the acid chamber larger than the gas chamber. This arrangement allows the back pressure of gas to force the acid down into the acid chamber, compressing the air in the acid chamber without permitting any gas to find its way into the acid chamber and thus preventing a waste of gas. In this horizontal partition and over the pendent pipe a number of ¼-inch holes are drilled or punched. This enables the acid to pass freely into the gas chamber, and prevents any small particles of zinc from falling into the acid chamber, which would generate gas in the chamber. Connected to the top of this acid chamber is a small pipe which runs up through the gas chamber and terminates above it, as shown. This pipe has an air inlet valve, or small hose end gas cock, connected into the side of the pipe, to which the hose from the force pump is attached when supplying air to the acid chamber to force from the acid chamber to the gas chamber in order to start the generation of gas. A safety or blow off valve is also attached to this pipe at the top, and is set to an ordinary working pressure of 15 pounds, or to any pressure desired. If gas is being generated faster than is required it gets up a pressure in excess of 15 pounds. Then the safety valve opens and allows the air in the acid chamber to escape until the gas goes down to the desired pressure again. This obviously allows a portion of the acid to return to the acid chamber, and later, as the acid becomes weaker, the air in this chamber will have to be renewed by the admission of a little more air.

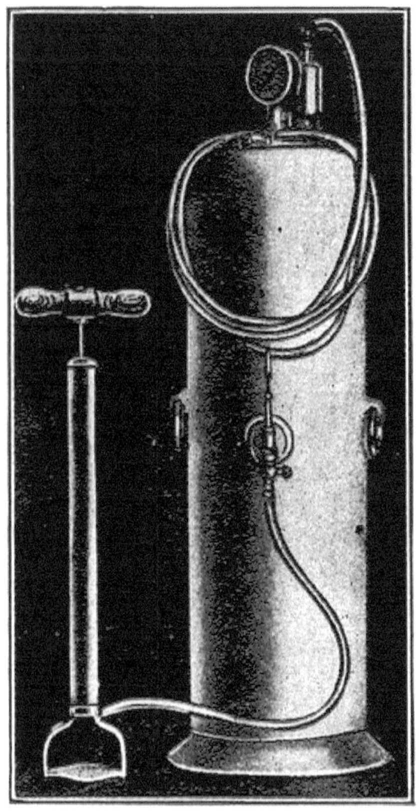

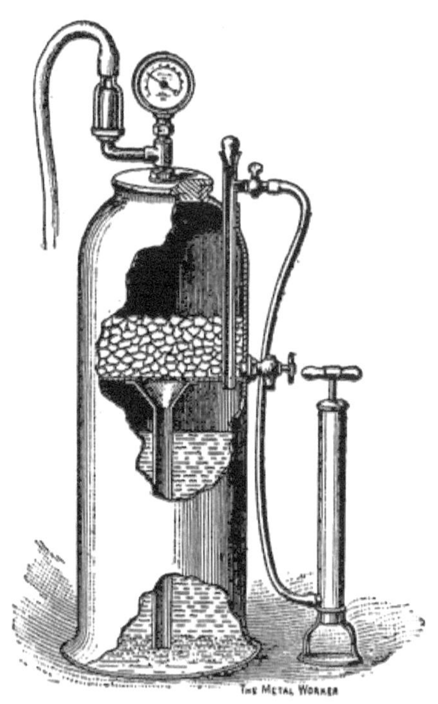

FIG. 44.—GENERAL VIEW.   FIG. 45.—SECTIONAL VIEW.
THE KIRKWOOD LEAD BURNING MACHINE.

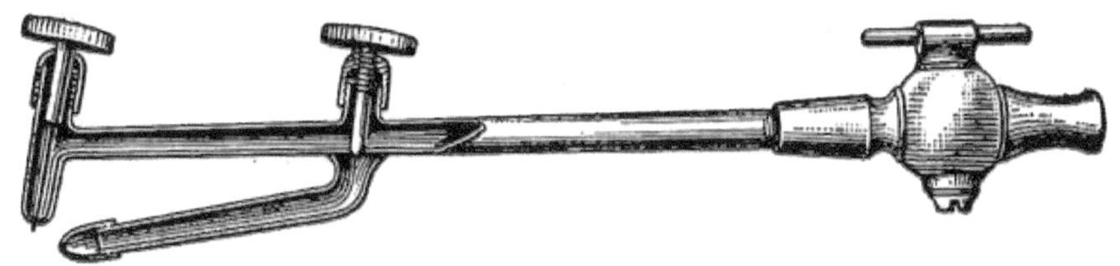

FIG. 46.—THE KIRKWOOD LEAD BURNER.

A large charging screw is placed directly in the top of the gas chamber. Into this is screwed a tee and short nipple, or it may be a special fitting made for that purpose. On this tee or special fitting a pressure gauge is screwed, and a float valve is attached on the branch. Into the gas chamber or as close to the partition as possible an angle valve is placed.

To Operate.

To charge the apparatus the safety valve is removed and the amount of the charge of acidulated water having been previously ascertained, the charge is poured into the acid chamber through the air pipe. The charge of spelter or zinc is placed in the gas chamber through the charging screw on top of the gas chamber. The pump is now attached to the air inlet cock with a short hose, and a few strokes of the pump will force the acid up into the gas chamber until the zinc is completely submerged. The generation of gas will begin at once.

The cock on the burner is then closed until the necessary working pressure is obtained, when it is ready for use. The pressure of gas can be regulated by setting the safety valve to blow off at a greater or less pressure, as desired. The use of the float valve is to prevent acid from being forced out of the gas chamber and into the tube. If this happens, the valve floats up and instantly closes the outlet, in which condition the valve remains until sufficient gas is generated to force the acid back into the acid chamber. When first charging the machine, acid should be forced up into the gas chamber until this valve closes, as that will force all of the air contained in the gas chamber out through the tube, leaving only pure gas in the generator. When the acid is spent it is easily removed from the generator by attaching the pump to the air inlet cock and forcing the acid up into the gas chamber. The angle valve is then opened, when the spent acid can be drawn off into a pail or other receptacle. This will not drain the acid chamber absolutely dry, but practically so.

When the operator ceases work, as for dinner or for any purpose, all that is necessary is to open the air inlet cock and detach the hose from the gas outlet. The acid will return by gravity to the acid chamber when generation ceases. When the operator is ready to resume work a few strokes of the pump will start generation again.

The Burner.

The burner, shown in Fig. 46, which is the most important part of the apparatus, is also constructed on a principle not heretofore used on a lead burning apparatus. It consists of a small tube, to one end of which is screwed a small cock, similar to a pet cock. To the other end, at a convenient angle, is brazed the burner proper. This consists of a needle point valve. The needle point, being about ½ inch long, is arranged so that the point can pass through the gas outlet about 1-16 inch. This seems to spread the flame in such a manner that it absorbs sufficient air to reduce the flame. It can be regulated by drawing the needle in or out, as the work requires. There is also a tube arranged to act as a by-pass or subflame. By opening the valve on this by-pass a pilot or subflame is maintained, which does away with the annoyance of having the flame pop out or become extinguished, as it is instantly ignited again by the subflame. In operating, the flame is held at such a distance from the work as experience will teach to be proper, or until the lead starts to melt. It should fuse with that well-known and instantly recognized bright appearance which indicates the nonoxidizing flame.

Any one who is used to handling the blow pipe can easily familiarize himself with this blow pipe. The maker claims that 2 quarts of vitriol will serve to operate the apparatus for a day of 8 hours on lead as heavy as 12-pound. I have no doubt that it will do even more than the makers claim for it. The apparatus is made in three sizes, adapted for different classes of work. After the experience I have had with it, I feel sure that any beginner can use this apparatus safely if he uses ordinary judgment and care in handling a gas apparatus that needs common sense treatment.

CHAPTER XIII.

SOFT SOLDERING WITH THE MOUTH BLOW PIPE.

The common blow pipe is a simple little tool that is used in connection with an alcohol torch for soldering the finest and most delicate pieces of jewelry, and constitutes the sole method of soldering used by Britannia workers and jewelers, and the fact that such a varied assortment of articles are soldered by the blow pipe process leads one to surmise that it can be used to advantage on coarser work. Though it is a familiar tool to gas fitters, plumbers as a rule are ignorant of its use, and it is hard work to find one who ever saw a blow pipe used on lead work. It is an easy matter to become proficient in its use, and the trick of keeping up a steady blast, and breathing regularly at the same time, is soon learned, and, when once acquired, stays with you always. This trick consists of making a bellows of your cheeks and using your tongue as a valve to close the entrance to the throat, leaving the passage from the nostrils to the lungs clear for breathing purposes. The only things necessary to purchase for practice are a common bent blow pipe, which can be had for about 15 cents, and a common candle.

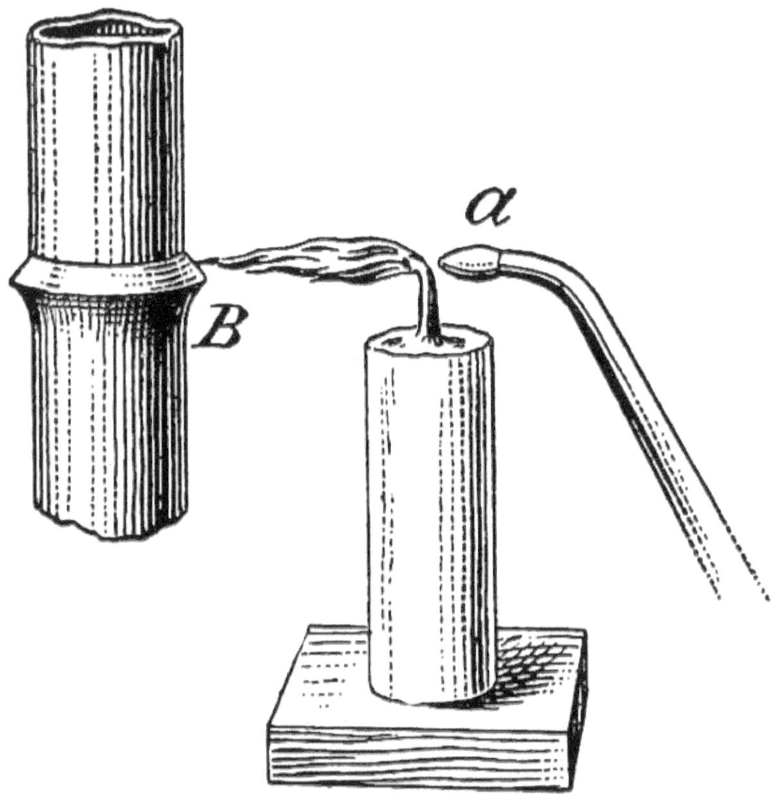

FIG. 47.—POSITION OF CANDLE AND BLOW PIPE.

To operate: The candle should be lighted, and when it burns well and freely the tip of the blow pipe should be brought close to the flame and slightly above the wick, *a*, Fig. 45. Then blow lightly through the blow pipe, and a pointed clear blue flame from 1 to 2 inches long, which will burn paper or char wood at a distance of 6 or 8 inches from the flame, will be the result. The flame is hottest and best when it shows a perfect cone-shaped blaze, and is obtained by a very moderate blast. The variation of the blaze can be noted by commencing to blow very lightly and increasing the pressure gradually. The flame will then show all stages from a smoky flame to a long blaze that cannot be concentrated on any small surface. The little sharp tip is where the hydrogen burns, and is the hottest part of the flame, being the part that is used for soldering.

Now, having noted these peculiarities, and knowing the perfect flame by sight, we will proceed to acquire the steady blast. The blow pipe should be held between the lips, which will form a tight packing around it, and must not come in contact with the teeth. The cheeks are then inflated, which will have a tendency to throw the tongue back to the throat and prevent the air in the mouth from blowing out through the nose. Now, by contracting the cheeks, and throwing the tongue slowly forward, the air will be forced through the blow pipe. This action is assisted when exhaling air by the pressure of the lungs, but when inhaling air the muscular contraction of the cheeks is depended upon entirely for the blast.

The ability to keep up a steady blast is merely a trick, or knack, and is learned with a few hours' practice; when learned, the length of time that the blast can be kept up depends solely upon the strength of the muscles of the cheeks of the operator. If these did not tire, the blast could be kept up for an indefinite time. Having learned to keep up the steady blast and get a perfect flame, the beginner will want to practice soldering. The blow pipe method of soldering has for its range of work everything that can be soldered, from Britannia metal to platinum, but the only metals that are used by the plumbers are tin and lead and their several compositions, so we will confine ourselves to the study of those metals.

Kinds of Solder Used.

In soldering any metal the solder should be so proportioned that it will melt many degrees lower in temperature than the metal to be soldered. Otherwise it would be quite probable that holes would be burned in the work before the solder would melt. There are exceptions to this rule, however; for example, lead burning, where one piece of lead is fused to another. As also with Britannia metal, it can be, and is, soldered with its own material, but it would be likely to have holes burned in it occasionally, and to avoid this a solder mixed for that purpose should be prepared. Two receipts are given here for quick melting solders that are suitable for this work. The first is preferred, but the second will answer the purpose.

Solder No. 1: Procure 4 ounces of pure lead, 4 ounces of pure tin, and 2 ounces of bismuth. The lead should be melted first and thoroughly stirred and cleaned. It should then be allowed to cool to the melting temperature of the tin, which should then be added. Lastly add the bismuth. The whole should then be stirred and poured into a suitable mold into very thin strips, about the size of a No. 8 wire, making strips of solder that can be rolled up and carried in the pocket.

Solder No. 2: This solder is composed of two parts of tin and one part of lead. These should be mixed as described above. To have success in making solders several points must be observed. The metal melting at the highest temperature should be melted first, which must then be allowed to drop to the melting temperature of the next metal to be added, and when ready to pour into molds the mixture must be stirred, as the specific gravity of the several metals differs considerably, and unless constant stirring is resorted to the mixture will partially separate upon cooling, and the result is an irregular solder that will not do the work.

Practicing the Blowing.

Now, for practice, take two pieces of ¼-inch lead tubing and prepare them as for a cup joint, by spreading one end with the bending iron and rasping the other end to fit the cup, as shown in *a*, Fig. 33. Support them as you best can in an upright position. Flux the joint with rosin. Then take the solder in the left hand, set the lighted candle at the right hight and distance from the joint, as shown at B,

Fig. 47, which leaves the right hand free to manage the blow pipe. Then heat the joint with the flame, and, as it gets hot, touch the joint with the solder, and when it reaches the melting temperature of the solder a drop of it will detach itself and flow clear around the joint, making a smooth, clean joint that is stronger than the pipe itself.

Joints made in this manner present a handsome and workmanlike appearance to the mechanical eye. Practice diligently on the lead pipe until you have become so proficient that you can flow the solder all through the joint without withdrawing the flame. Then procure some ⅜-inch block tin pipe, and, when that can be soldered perfectly, the beginner can consider himself sufficiently proficient to practice on flat seams on Britannia metal.

Soldering Britannia Metal.

For working Britannia metal the candle cannot be used, as the dripping grease will cover the work and seriously interfere with the flowing solder. The beginner must provide himself with an alcohol or kerosene torch. A good form of torch, manufactured and sold for electricians' use, is shown in Fig. 48. The alcohol gives a clean flame, but by comparison is somewhat expensive. The kerosene gives a flame that can be concentrated on a small surface with fully as much heat, and if care is taken to allow only the blue flame to touch the work, it is fully as clean and cheaper.

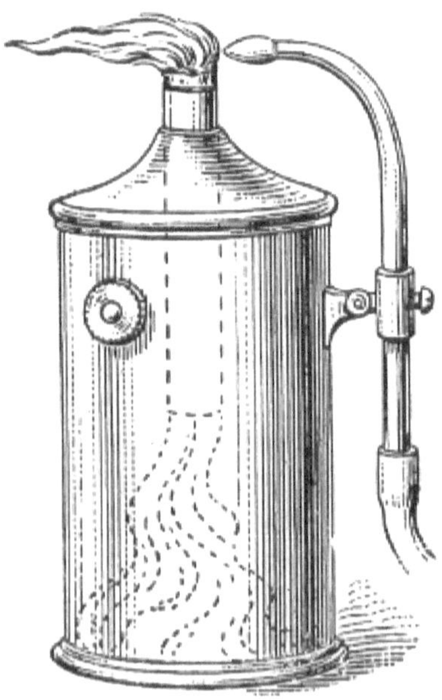

FIG. 48.—ALCOHOL OR KEROSENE TORCH.

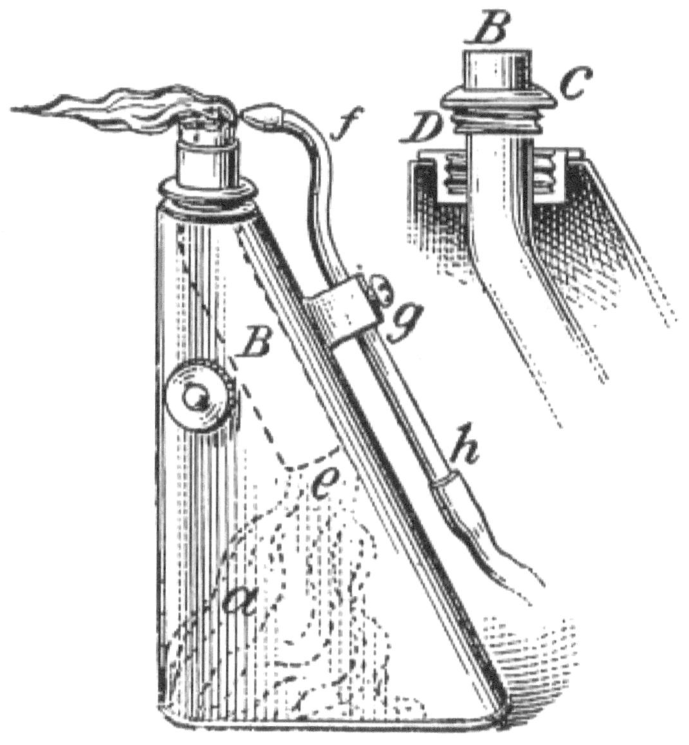

FIG. 49.—A SPECIALLY CONSTRUCTED TORCH.

The burning kerosene torch gives off a dirty smell and smoke, which makes it disagreeable to handle, but this is a case of take your choice, and it is left to the beginner to use either, as they will both do the work satisfactorily. It is also necessary, in doing this work, to have the blow pipe attached to the torch and connected to the mouth with a piece of very small rubber tube. This will leave one hand free to apply the flux and hold the solder. The flame can also be quickly placed in any position or directed to any portion of the work without allowing the work to cool. The alcohol torch for this work should be so constructed that it can be held in a horizontal or inverted position without spilling the contents of the torch.

The handiest, as also the cheapest, torch to make is the one shown in Fig. 49. It consists of a can 3 inches high made in the shape of a frustum of a scalene cone. The tube B should be ¼ inch in diameter, and must run parallel with the flaring side and extend half way to the bottom of the can, as *e*. Then, when the torch is tipped to solder horizontal work, the alcohol will flow into the space *a*, leaving the alcohol to supply the wick to be drawn up by capillary attraction. This tube is made of ¼-inch brass tubing, bent to form an angle with the can, as shown.

FIG. 50.—USING THE TORCH ON A FLAT SEAM.

A screw and cap with a seat, such as is used on brass lamps, is obtained, and a hole punched in the cap *c* just large enough to receive the tube B. The screw is soldered into the opening of the can at D. The wick, which is formed of many strands of candle wicking rolled tightly together, is pulled through the tube by means of a wire hook, and left sufficiently long to lie in the space *a*, so that it will always lie in the alcohol. This tube is placed through the hole at D, and allowed to project about ¾ inch outside of the can. Wicking is then wound around the tube and forced into the socket formed in the screw D. The cap is then slipped over the tube at *c*, and screwed down tight on the wicking, which will make a tight joint at D, and will hold the tube firmly in place.

When necessary to fill the torch the tube can easily be removed and the torch filled. A separate filling screw can be used if desired. Even with this form of torch an excess of alcohol will occasionally get into the wick when used in a horizontal position and increase the size of the blaze. But when this happens the torch can be brought to an upright position for a moment, which will drain the wick and bring the blaze to its proper size.

The blow pipe for this torch is made from a piece of very small copper or brass tubing. The end intended for the tip should be bent to the angle required, as shown at *f*, Fig. 49. It should be fastened to the torch by means of a clamp, *g*, soldered to the flaring side of the torch. This clamp should be so arranged that the blow pipe can be adjusted to the requirements of the blaze. This clamp consists of a short piece of brass. A hole is drilled in one end to allow the blow pipe to pass through, while the other end is filed to fit the bevel of the can to which it is soldered. The blow pipe can be held in position with a wedge, or a hole can be drilled and tapped and a small screw inserted which will hold the blow pipe firmly in place. The tip of the blow pipe should not be larger than 1-32 inch. The rubber tube can then be attached to the projecting end of the blow pipe at *h*, which is then ready for use.

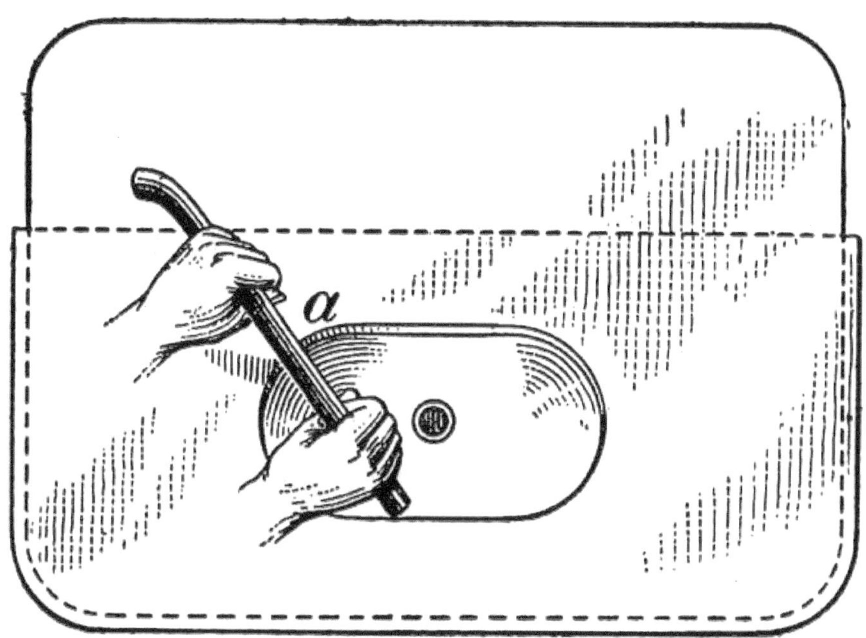

FIG. 51.—CUTTING METAL FOR A BUTLER'S PANTRY SINK.

Owing to the Britannia metal melting at such a low temperature, it would be well for the beginner to practice on pieces of 2-pound sheet lead. Seams on this class of work are made by butting the edges of the metal, as these seams are not supposed to show. The seams are prepared by truing the edges and then beveling the edges with the shave hook so that when brought together a V-shaped groove is formed. This is then fluxed with a small amount of powdered rosin. A drop of the quick melting solder is then melted from the strip and allowed to drop on the seam. The flame is then applied to the sheets, and as the solder flows the flame must be kept slightly in advance of it, Fig. 50. Care must be taken to heat the sheets only enough to cause the solder to flow. Otherwise the seam will not appear full. The beginner should experience no trouble in soldering these lead seams, and when perfect control of the torch and flame is had, pieces of Britannia metal should be substituted for the lead. These seams are prepared and fluxed just as for lead.

Britannia metal is fast becoming the favorite lining for splash and drip boards on butler's pantry sinks, as also for lining the work benches in saloons. It is soft enough to allow the most delicate china to be laid on it without danger of chipping, and is also very easy to keep clean. It takes a high polish and always looks well. The method of cutting the metal for a butler's pantry sink is shown in Fig. 51, the dotted lines showing the actual dimensions of the article to be covered, while the full lines show the laps required to cover the edges of the board. This metal is harder than lead, and will not dress smooth with the dresser. Any uneven spots must be pressed down with a hot flatiron. The method of turning the edges is shown at *a*. The bending iron is heated and rubbed over the edge, gradually turning the edges until they are at their proper position. The iron must be constantly heated to insure the best results, and if properly done no wrinkles will appear. A lined work bench is also shown in Fig. 52, which shows the method of putting in the bar washer. The sheet metal must be cut and fitted to its place and all the seams possible should be soldered before placing the metal in position. The edges should be tacked on the under side of the work, when practicable, with copper tacks.

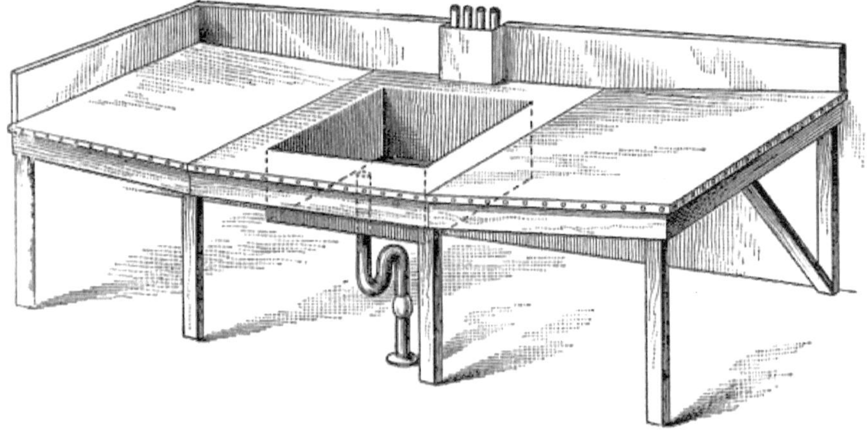

FIG. 52.—A LINED WORK BENCH, WITH BAR WASHER.

Sooner or later the blow pipe solderer will be called upon to make repairs on Britannia metal, and will be surprised to find that it will be impossible to solder the metal, owing to the excess of moisture under it. The best way to overcome this, which is practically the only trouble that occurs, is to cut out a small square patch. The edge can be cleaned and a patch of new metal carefully fitted into the hole. When ready to begin soldering, a piece of blotting paper should be inserted between the patch and board. This paper will absorb all the moisture and allow the seam to be neatly soldered. The man who makes himself familiar with the blow pipe and torch soon finds himself in a different class from the ordinary everyday mechanic, and if mechanical ability be accompanied with sobriety and stability, the possessor will always command a good steady income.

THE END.

INDEX

Lector House believes that a society develops through a two-fold approach of continuous learning and adaptation, which is derived from the study of classic literary works spread across the historic timeline of literature records. Therefore, we aim at reviving, repairing and redeveloping all those inaccessible or damaged but historically as well as culturally important literature across subjects so that the future generations may have an opportunity to study and learn from past works to embark upon a journey of creating a better future.

This book is a result of an effort made by Lector House towards making a contribution to the preservation and repair of original ancient works which might hold historical significance to the approach of continuous learning across subjects.

HAPPY READING & LEARNING!

LECTOR HOUSE LLP
E-MAIL: lectorpublishing@gmail.com